D1608400

WHAT WORKS IN
TALENT DEVELOPMENT

Effective Onboarding

Norma Dávila and
Wanda Piña-Ramírez

© 2018 ASTD DBA the Association for Talent Development (ATD)
All rights reserved. Printed in the United States of America.

21 20 19 18   1 2 3 4 5

No part of this publication may be reproduced, distributed, or transmitted in any form or by any means, including photocopying, recording, information storage and retrieval systems, or other electronic or mechanical methods, without the prior written permission of the publisher, except in the case of brief quotations embodied in critical reviews and certain other noncommercial uses permitted by copyright law. For permission requests, please go to www.copyright.com, or contact Copyright Clearance Center (CCC), 222 Rosewood Drive, Danvers, MA 01923 (telephone: 978.750.8400; fax: 978.646.8600).

ATD Press is an internationally renowned source of insightful and practical information on talent development, training, and professional development.

ATD Press
1640 King Street
Alexandria, VA 22314 USA

Ordering information: Books published by ATD Press can be purchased by visiting ATD's website at www.td.org/books or by calling 800.628.2783 or 703.683.8100.

Library of Congress Control Number: 2018950351

ISBN-10: 1-947308-60-2
ISBN-13: 978-1-947308-60-2
e-ISBN: 978-1-947308-61-9

ATD Press Editorial Staff
Director: Kristine Luecker
Manager: Melissa Jones
Community of Practice Manager, Human Capital: Eliza Blanchard
Developmental Editor: Kathryn Stafford
Text Design: Shirley E.M. Raybuck
Cover Design: Shirley E.M. Raybuck

Printed by Versa Press, East Peoria, IL

Your name should be here…

…because you shared your story.
…because you spent time with us.
…because you talked about your challenges and successes.
…because you challenged our wisdom and respected our ignorance.
…because we grew with you.
…because you imprinted every single one of these pages.
…because now we know "What Works" in onboarding.

This book is for you.

Contents

About the Series

ATD's What Works in Talent Development series addresses the most critical topics facing today's talent development practitioners. Each book in the series is written for trainers, by trainers, and offers a clear and defined pathway to solving real issues. Interwoven with the latest findings in technology and best practices, this series is designed to enhance your current efforts on core subject matter, while offering a practical guide for you to follow. Authored by seasoned experts, each book is jammed packed with easy-to-apply content—including job aids, checklists, and other reference materials—to make the learning transfer process simple.

The What Works in Talent Development series is a unique core collection designed for talent development practitioners at every career level. To date, the books in the series include:

- *Starting a Talent Development Program*
- *Blended Learning*
- *Effective Onboarding*

Introduction

Onboarding is a business driver that ensures your company's new or new-to-role employees are the right fit. After employees are hired or brought into a new role, onboarding is the critical step connecting them with the organizational culture and their roles. In some cases, onboarding can be considered the first element of employee retention.

Employee onboarding is often misconstrued as a synonym for new employee orientation. Even though the second is part of the first, they serve different purposes in the employee's employment life cycle. Effective onboarding programs significantly affect employee engagement and employee branding, which is generally defined as how employees internalize the brand that the business showcases and align their behaviors and perspectives with it. Understanding the common misconceptions between employee orientation and onboarding is critical to defining the goals and scope of your own onboarding program. Clarifying these concepts will assist you as you build your business case and communicate to others why onboarding is important and how they can contribute to its results for every new and new-to-role employee.

Starting during recruitment and selection, employee onboarding is a more encompassing experience, crucial for both the employee and the business. Defining when onboarding starts will help you establish program timelines while securing the participation of the players, such as program facilitators, who add value to the program. Explaining what will happen and when will ease the transitions of those involved, which then benefits the onboarding program participants, hiring managers, and the business.

Companies need to know when the employee who participates in onboarding will be ready to become a productive business contributor. As you design or revise your onboarding program—based on the results of your organizational analysis and supported with current best practices—you will be able to ascertain a more accurate program ending point, thus strengthening your position and your business case.

Time considerations are a critical element of program design. In the case of onboarding, program duration is not clear cut, although the process can take around a year. Therefore, understanding the nuances of onboarding programs will help allay unrealistic expectations about what the program will achieve and by when.

Another common misconception about onboarding is that it is the sole responsibility of the organization's human resources department when, in fact, it is a multiprong effort shared among different stakeholders at different times. Onboarding also is not limited to new hires. Research has shown that role clarification in onboarding, beyond the discussion of job descriptions and focusing on role expectations, is a critical factor for program success. Talya N. Bauer's 2013 survey of more than 12,000 new employees found that role clarification was one of the most important components of onboarding because it was related to employee performance. Her interviews, observations, and further research confirmed that role clarity is paramount for employee success.

Investing in onboarding is investing in employee success, which subsequently translates into investing in the business's future. Effective onboarding programs significantly increase and facilitate business results, employee engagement, and employee branding because they focus on how the employee's role contributes to move the organization forward and deliver desired outcomes.

Consider the following facts:

- According to a 2016 study by the Human Capital Institute:
  - » 78 percent of companies that invest in onboarding report the "continuation of a positive candidate experience," 69 percent report "easier assimilation into the company culture," 67 percent claim employees have a "clear understanding of performance expectations," 61 percent found "increased engagement levels," and 60 percent indicated "decreased time to proficiency."
  - » 47 percent of those surveyed agree with the statement, "Our onboarding program speeds up time to proficiency for new hires."
  - » 20 percent of new hires leave their companies within the first 45 days (Filipkowski 2016).
- A 2017 study among HR leaders in the United States conducted by Kronos and HCI found that:

» Three-quarters of survey respondents believed onboarding practices were underutilized.

» Nearly a quarter of organizations had no onboarding strategy or process for internal hires.

» Just over a third of companies had insufficient technology to automate or organize the onboarding process.

» 47 percent of those surveyed stated that onboarding programs were successful at retaining new hires (Filipkowski, Heinsch, and Wiete 2017).

Thus, establishing a solid, sustainable onboarding program makes sense for the future of the business.

About This Book

Effective Onboarding describes how to design, implement, and evaluate an onboarding program; demonstrate its success; and sustain it for the future. Time is a valuable resource in every business because its use has a direct impact on profitability. This book aims to shorten the time that you need to design, revise, or expand your company's onboarding program. It is based on what we have learned as talent development practitioners about onboarding best practices from clients in diverse industries, cultures, and sizes.

Regardless of your role in your company's onboarding program—whether you are revising the existing program, expanding its scope to include internal promotions, or evaluating the current program's success—you will find valuable tools and information in these pages to meet your needs. Even if your company is satisfied with the results of its current onboarding program, you may gain a new perspective on what you could add or modify to make it even better as part of your company's continuous improvement efforts.

Effective Onboarding combines our experiences and the latest onboarding trends to create a single source where you can find examples, job aids, models, templates, and checklists of what you need to do to take immediate action to get results. We encourage you to read the entire book to gain a broad understanding of the onboarding process. We then suggest that you go back to those chapters that are particularly relevant for your own project. You could also tailor the tools and templates related to your current onboarding program's pain points to meet your needs. Thought-provoking questions are included to help you design, revise, or expand your own program.

Our examples and stories are based on real-life situations that we have encountered in our practice; they showcase best practices and pitfalls to avoid. The lists of additional resources will also help to expand your options as you work to address your program's specific needs.

Chapter by Chapter Overview

Each of the books in the What Works in Talent Development series follows a similar framework. The chapters in this book discuss what onboarding is, why it's important, how to design it, how to implement it, how to evaluate the outcome, and what you can do to prepare for the future of learning.

Chapter 1: Getting Started describes what onboarding is and is not. It introduces the importance of employee onboarding for the organization and why businesses should onboard all their employees—whether they are new to the company or new to a role. After reading this chapter, you will be ready to identify the different potential audiences for your onboarding program, such as new and new-to-role employees, as well as the multiple stakeholders, such as senior management and boards of directors, who will participate.

Chapter 2: Shaping the Future highlights the impact of employee onboarding on organizations, discussing in detail the benefits of onboarding programs for the business, employees, and managers. After reading this chapter, you will be able to avoid the pitfalls that cause many onboarding programs to fail.

Chapter 3: Designing Your Onboarding Program takes you through the five phases of beginning to design your organization's onboarding program: assessing the current state, defining the desired state, analyzing the gap, closing the gap, and building the business case for onboarding. You will find guiding questions and templates to prompt your thinking and organize the information you collect for each phase so that you can make compelling arguments to support your recommendations about the onboarding program.

Chapter 4: Implementing the Plan takes the high-level design that you introduced in your business case into an actionable sequence of steps to revise or design your company's onboarding program. The chapter describes what to include to address the need that you defined during your organizational snapshot and gap analysis, whether your program is for new or new-to-role employees. You'll learn about different onboarding situations, such as for an individual contributor, manager, executive, or remote employee. You will also see how to use and adapt tools for your program—such as criteria to select buddies, mentors, and external coaches as well as sample letters and agendas—for general and role-specific onboarding.

Chapter 5: Transferring Learning and Evaluating Results describes the importance of measurement and evaluation, and how you can use return on investment (ROI) among other indicators to justify and sustain your program. You will be able to make any changes to the program that the business may require based on the information that you collect and analyze. We also explain the difference between the terms *measure, measurement,* and *evaluation,* which are often used interchangeably. At the end of the chapter, we suggest measures that you may use for your program.

Chapter 6: Planning Next Steps discusses program sustainability, which is the next step in reinforcing the importance of onboarding for the business. This chapter considers additional barriers to program success, such as underestimating the employee's learning curve and lack of support, with specific recommendations about how to overcome them. Included are examples of professional development activities that you can implement to keep onboarded employees on a continuous development path.

Given this book's brevity and its complex topic, we are assuming that you:

- are familiar with the ADDIE model and the Kirkpatrick evaluation framework
- have knowledge about recruitment and selection
- are aware of company expectations about new employee performance
- understand the business strategy
- can work easily with different company levels
- know about employee engagement
- understand organizational learning and transitions
- know about your company's approach to employee socialization
- know about SMART goals
- can deliver different types of messages
- are at ease managing different types of technology
- are comfortable giving and receiving feedback.

Icons Used in This Book

Throughout this book, you will find icons highlighting concepts and ideas introduced in the text.

Icon	What It Means
	Tips From Professionals will make your job easier and give you ideas to help apply the techniques and approaches discussed.
	Tools identify templates, checklists, worksheets, models, outlines, examples, illustrations, and other prototypes that can be a useful place to start.
	Resources are the books, blogs, articles, or even people that you can access to add to the information you have gained already and take your learning deeper.

Additional Resources

Bauer, T.N. 2013. *Onboarding: Enhancing New Employee Clarity and Confidence.* SuccessFactors Whitepaper. www.successfactors.com/en_us/download.html?a=/content /dam/successfactors/en_us/resources/white-papers/onboarding-employee -clarity-confidence.pdf.

Filipkowski, J. 2016. *Onboarding Outcomes: Fulfill New Hire Expectations.* Human Capital Institute, June 22. www.hci.org/hr-research/onboarding-outcomes-fulfill-new -hire-expectations.

Filipkowski, J., M.F. Heinsch, and A. Wiete. 2017. *New Hire Momentum: Driving the Onboarding Experience.* Signature Series, an HCI Insight Partnership. www.hci.org /files/field_content_file/2017%20Kronos_0.pdf.

Maurer, R. 2015. "Onboarding Key to Retaining, Engaging Talent." SHRM, April 16. www.shrm.org/resourcesandtools/hr-topics/talent-acquisition/pages/onboarding -key-retaining-engaging-talent.aspx.

———. 2018. "Employers Risk Driving New Hires Away With Poor Onboarding." SHRM, February 23. www.shrm.org/resourcesandtools/hr-topics/talent -acquisition/pages/employers-new-hires-poor-onboarding.aspx.

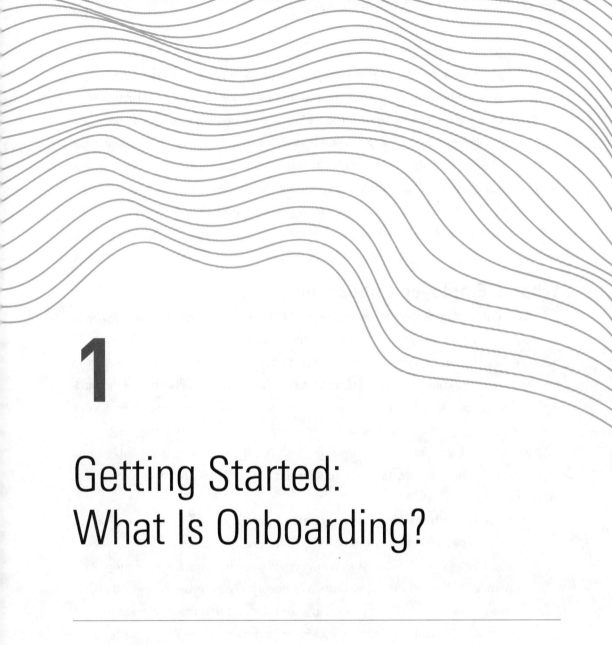

1

Getting Started: What Is Onboarding?

In This Chapter

- Defining onboarding
- Clarifying the differences between orientation and onboarding
- Importance of onboarding
- Stakeholders of onboarding

Talent development professionals sometimes tell us that new employees complain about not getting the resources they need to succeed or that their expectations did not match the reality of the organization. Others have said that new employees left their organizations because they were confused about what they needed to do. We also hear complaints from managers about new employees not being the right fit or not being capable enough for the challenge that they were expected to meet. What went wrong? These employees probably never went through the right onboarding, or there was a mismatch between the onboarding program and their reality.

What Is Employee Onboarding?

Employee onboarding is the process through which companies engage new employees or new-to-role employees in the company's culture and with their role. This process is designed to ease the movement of employees through the organizational threshold to become productive contributors and team members in the least possible time. Onboarding's influence on employee performance is company-wide. Therefore, it is directly connected to business outcomes and warrants a sizeable investment in resources.

Onboarding has two distinct yet complementary components: general onboarding and role-specific onboarding. General onboarding is more prevalent than role-specific onboarding.

- **General onboarding** introduces the employee to the company's culture (how things are done) by establishing commonalities among all employees regardless of position, such as hourly employees, individual contributors, or managers. For instance, the company's history, vision, mission, and values, as well as overall policies, procedures, and dos and don'ts are relevant to everyone. Specialized training sessions required for all employees, such as how to complete human resources transactions or fill out a timesheet, are also part of general onboarding. This component of the process establishes the ground rules to engage newcomers with the workplace.

- **Role-specific onboarding** entails a uniquely tailored process for each position in the company because it seeks assimilation of the new or new-to-role employee into the nuances of the department's or unit's culture. This component helps the employees acquire the knowledge, skills, and behaviors they need to master the role effectively and efficiently and feel at ease performing at the expected levels in the shortest possible timeframe.

Regardless of industry or company size, activities are highly individualized for each position and require a transfer of knowledge from the learning and development function to the manager or immediate supervisor, who will lead the process from that point.

Origins of Onboarding Programs

As organizations and jobs became more complex, businesses realized that they needed to provide a starting point for their employees, whether new to the company or new to their roles, to perform their jobs. Companies began experimenting with different practices until they found what seemed to be effective for them. Some based those practices on organizational socialization approaches, which, according to Georgia T. Chao (2012), is "a learning and adjustment process that enables an individual to assume an organizational role that fits both organizational and individual needs." In other words, it is what the company does to help a new employee acquire the required behaviors to succeed within the company and adjust to its culture and their role in it.

The preferences of the company's country of origin may also influence how companies refer to activities such as new hire training, new employee assimilation, employee adjustment, or employee induction. However, *onboarding* is the most commonly used and accepted way in businesses to refer to these processes today.

PRO TIP

Make sure that managers know the difference between socialization into the organization and socializing in the organization.

Differences Between Employee Orientation and Employee Onboarding

Orientation and onboarding jointly set the stage for the journey across the employee life cycle. One is the beginning of the other, and both create that fundamental first impression. You need to make onboarding matter, regardless of the type and size of your business. Employee orientation should be part of the employee onboarding process (Figure 1-1).

Figure 1-1. Relationship Between Employee Orientation and Role-Specific Onboarding

The following two examples illustrate the differences between employee orientation and employee onboarding.

Marcia's Story

Marcia joined the sales team of a major telecommunications corporation after having a successful career as a sales representative for a global pharmaceutical manufacturing company. She has seven years of experience in direct sales and was enticed by the challenge of starting in a new industry. Her new employer has a solid reputation for its customer service approach and high-quality products. Marcia eagerly accepted the offer, which included a significant salary increase and benefits.

Marcia arrived at the company's main office ready to start the next stage of her career. To her surprise, her new manager was out of town. After she waited in the lobby for about an hour, the human resources representative who recruited her brought the paperwork she needed to complete before she could start. Marcia spent about two hours reading and signing documents. When it was time for lunch, someone told her to go find something to eat on her own. When she returned, she attended a four-hour group session, where she heard several talks about the past, present, and future of the company, as well as the rules that all employees needed to follow. At the end of the session, she received an employee handbook and information about company policies. She was also told to report to a general sales training the following morning.

The telecommunications company did not provide onboarding; they only provided a general orientation. Marcia felt lost.

Justin's Story

Justin accepted an offer to become supervisor of a consumer credit call center. Justin had previously worked as a call center supervisor for a medical insurance company. His new job requires him to supervise a team of 35 employees who collect payments from customers or obtain commitments to pay. Justin learned as much as he could about his new company from its website and industry-related publications as well as from the interview process, where someone was always ready to answer his questions. He completed all the paperwork related to his new position before his first day.

When Justin arrived at his new workplace, the receptionist greeted him by name and so did other employees who happened to be there. His manager introduced Justin to his new team and spent the rest of the morning discussing the schedule for the week. Justin learned that he would attend a general orientation session with other new employees followed by a customized monthlong program that his manager would facilitate to ensure his assimilation into the company and his role. He received a welcome letter from his colleagues, his ID was ready for him, the T-shirt he was given to wear at the company's gym was the correct size; he also received an invite to join any of the company's social responsibility groups. Justin felt supported and valued in the organization; he had a clear sense of direction about where he was going in the company from the start.

Marcia and Justin had two completely different experiences during their first day at their new organizations. Marcia received a typical new employee orientation, one full of information and paperwork instead of an onboarding process. Her experience illustrates what companies should not do. In contrast, Justin had a planned formal experience that was tailored to meet his needs and directed at his integration and success. His new organization was ready to receive him and focus on what really matters.

Marcia's first day at work involved completing forms and signing documents that, although important and often required by law, did not contribute to her understanding of the company or her role. The facts, figures, and rules presented in the group session were all useful to know; however, unless they are placed in the proper context, they do not add value to the new employee's development. Further, the absence of her manager and the requirement to attend a general sales training session, despite being an experienced salesperson already, turned an otherwise noteworthy opportunity for the organization to create a positive first impression into one more event to be checked off a list. Marcia was required to attend the training session to comply with a requirement, regardless of her experience or what she could contribute. Her first day at work was memorable because it was uninspiring.

In contrast, Justin completed administrative tasks and started building relationships with his new manager and fellow employees before his first day. He felt welcomed upon arrival and immediately began to build on his rapport with his manager through their formal and informal conversations about the plans for the next month. Meeting his new team and later attending group sessions initiated that important integration process into the company culture. Learning that the organization had an individualized program in place that valued his background and his potential to contribute to the organization provided a sense of belonging and engagement that cannot be overlooked.

Different Types of Programs to Serve Different Purposes

The programs that organizations offer to their new employees vary widely. While some are as short term and general as Marcia's, others are more customized like Justin's. While many organizations refer to these programs as new employee orientation or new employee onboarding interchangeably, Marcia's and Justin's examples illustrate how distinct the two experiences are and the very different objectives they achieve. Marcia's experience is best described as a failed attempt at an employee orientation; Justin's is a good example of a successful employee onboarding program.

RESOURCE

In *Creative Onboarding Programs: Tools for Energizing Your Orientation Programs*, Doris M. Sims introduces examples of what businesses are currently doing to onboard their employees. Check it out to see if some of the examples could be useful for your program.

Employee Orientation

Employee orientation is a time-bound single event where most organizations assume that "one size fits all," often bringing together employees who perform different roles and functions whose main commonality is their effective date of hire. In these group sessions, led by L&D, a senior manager usually welcomes attendees either in person or using video or teleconferencing technology. L&D then leads the rest of the agenda, with appearances from human resources and other departments. In the absence of L&D, HR or the company's owners lead this process.

Employee orientations are usually structured as a series of separate presentations that, among other topics, highlight the company's history, present, values, and culture, as well as its vision for the future. These presentations, often held in classroom-type settings, are usually laden with policies, rules, and regulations employees must follow, along with the implicit message that they must do so to remain employed. Many companies integrate the use of technology in these orientations and even deliver some content through customized company apps. Sometimes attendees can complete paperwork or receive training about how to conduct transactions, such as requesting direct deposit of their wages, signing up for savings and retirement programs, or designating beneficiaries for life insurance.

PRO TIP

Ensure that employee orientation is relevant to the employee's level in the organization by providing examples of situations that are commonplace for the attendee's level. Schedule separate sessions for exempt and nonexempt employees.

Orientation programs vary in duration from several hours to several days and are increasingly delivered online. However, there is no substitute for direct personal contact—studies, such as those of Wesson and Gogus (2005), show that employees assimilate less and have less understanding of the company and the job when they receive only computer-based versions of onboarding.

Although useful, the information conveyed during employee orientations is, by design, far too general and only minimally achieves the goal of facilitating a new employee's transition to becoming an effective business contributor. Even though attendees value the opportunity to meet fellow employees, they object to information overload as well as the lack of information specifically related to their own roles. Therefore, when these employees arrive at their units, they have another "first day."

PRO TIP

Make your company's history real by providing examples that add value to the onboarders' experience. Asking them to read the information from a website is not enough.

Pre-Onboarding

Pre-onboarding comprises all the activities that take place before the new employee or new-to-role employee receives the employment offer. The organization's recruitment and selection activities are part of this component.

Pre-onboarding includes many steps and actions:

- Employee accepts employment offer letter.
- The employee receives additional information about the company.
- Paperwork related to the hiring process is completed.
- The company requests any necessary uniforms and personalized equipment for the employee.
- The arrival of the new employee is announced.
- The employee receives information prior to arrival to know what to expect.
- The company sends a welcome packet to the employee.
- The employee meets other employees informally.
- The employee starts becoming familiar with the new company's culture.

TOOL

The Pre-Onboarding Checklist located at the end of this chapter is useful to ensure completion of pre-onboarding tasks.

General Onboarding

Organizations begin to create that emotional connection between the employee and the company's purpose by discussing the company's mission, vision, and values and, most important, making them come alive for employees. When employees can relate to the company's mission, they construe their relationship with the organization as a more personal one. When they are aware of the company's vision, they see a future for themselves in the company. When their values and those of the company are congruent, employees do not experience the cognitive dissonance that often leads them to seek opportunities elsewhere.

Each company's culture, which defines how the business does what it does, is unique, and each locality within a company has its own culture. For example, subtle cultural differences between departments often exist within a company. Employees need to under-

Chapter

stand the company's culture because everything they do as well as how o
and reward what they do is embedded within that culture. Therefore, they n.
those critical written and unwritten cultural rules as soon as possible to be suc

Company brand, which is the essence of what the company stands for ..crnally
and externally and how it differentiates itself from the competition, is often one of the
factors that attracts a candidate to an organization. Thus, the company's internal and
external brands must be aligned—any discrepancies between them may influence an
employee's decision about staying or leaving. Employees represent the company and its
brand everywhere they go and in everything they do. In today's culture, anything can
get posted on social media, and a single incident can make or break a company's or
an employee's reputation, so creating that awareness of the company's brand from the
beginning gains additional significance.

The size and scope of the company's market, the group to whom the organization
delivers its goods and services and its distinguishing characteristics, influences whether
employees can see the impact of what they do locally, nationally, or internationally, and
how they envision the company's competitors. The size and scope of the market also
affect the complexity of the organization, which, in turn, may affect the complexity of
the employee's role and potential career path.

When employees can visualize the end users of the products and services their
companies offer, they become more personally invested in those products and services
as well as in how they see themselves representing the company and the brand. Thus,
introducing employees to the company customer base defines the company's market
even further.

The company's organizational structure serves to guide how they function internally by delineating reporting relationships and spans of control. In its graphic form, the
organizational structure portrays the complexity of the business, the formality of the
company, and the options for career mobility. Often presented as a living document,
the organizational structure is another mechanism for showing employees where they
fit within the business and linking the names, positions, and, possibly, faces of those
with whom they will interact more or less frequently.

Role-Specific Onboarding

Role-specific onboarding provides an employee multiple opportunities to assimilate
into the department's or unit's culture and master their new role.

General and tailored learning experiences allow employees to acquire specific technical skills and competencies unique to the new role. Companies may use a specific approach or a combination of approaches, such as traditional classroom training, on-the-job training, industry-specific publications, online courses, just-in-time learning tools, job shadowing, simulations, in-house or external academies, professional conferences, and immersion programs, as well as mentoring and coaching.

When employees attend company events, participate in meetings, partake in learning experiences, are present in the office, join internal and external client meetings, and interact informally with others, they expand their company networks as they initiate and build relationships with their manager or supervisor, peers, direct reports (if applicable), colleagues, and clients. By becoming members of professional organizations, they interact with other professionals in different settings while keeping their expertise up-to-date.

It is also important for employees to observe how their managers, supervisors, peers, direct reports (if applicable), colleagues, and clients communicate and interact with one another to learn about any unwritten rules that are crucial for a smooth role and cultural transition. Building an open and honest relationship with a buddy or mentor is a priceless way to gain additional insights into "how we do and don't do things around here," whether the employee just joined the organization or has moved to a completely different role that requires a different set of behaviors.

An onboarding program allows employees to grasp the magnitude of the company and its culture in general terms and to find their place in the company. Through onboarding, employees also find out how they fit in their department and how they can contribute to their department and to the business.

When defining the scope and duration of your organization's onboarding program, consider these factors:

- **Company industry.** Those industries that are highly regulated, such as banking, insurance, pharmaceutical manufacturing, construction, and hospitality, must abide by mandates and decrees that demand the inclusion of specific content in onboarding programs. Some industries, such as aeronautics manufacturing, do not allow employees to perform their jobs until they have undergone extensive training, demonstrated they can do the work independently, and been certified by an expert.

- **Company culture.** Culture can vary from very formal to laissez-faire. In formal company cultures, employees often have to follow a predetermined linear path and complete their onboarding within a particular timeframe; laissez-faire cultures often allow employees more flexibility to complete or even choose their programs. Learning about a formal company culture where employee behavior is completely prescribed will take longer than learning about an informal company culture where employees are encouraged to experiment and learn. Mistakes are not an option and can be costly within a formal company culture, while they may be encouraged in an informal company culture.

- **Reporting relationships.** These determine how employees interact with their supervisor or direct reports, and are easier to deal with when employees and supervisors are in the same place at the same time. However, employees may report to supervisors in a different location; if their contact is mostly electronic, they may rarely meet. Virtual or remote employees and supervisors have to define a different way of working and addressing issues than employees and supervisors who work in the same office. In onboarding, particularly in role-specific onboarding, companies should spell out the nuances of how to deal with these differences, as well as how to anticipate any potential roadblocks to success, because reporting relationships are so important to employee engagement, retention, and success.

- **Employee background.** This may be defined in demographic or educational terms. An organization needs to make sure that employees can work as part of a diverse workforce. Similarly, an organization has to account for any differences in educational level and the potential impact on employee interactions—between peers, between employees and supervisors, or among employees and supervisors with other levels of management—when tailoring role-specific onboarding to clarify all roles and relationships. For example, they need to determine the complexity of language and use of jargon, as well as the level of formality in alignment with company culture, depending on role and employee background.

- **Employee experience.** Components of role-specific onboarding have to acknowledge the employee's level of experience in terms of industry, role, tenure, and location as they relate to the position and expectations of the role. For example, the company's intention in selecting Candidate A, who has less experience in X, over Candidate B, who has more experience, has to be clear from the beginning. Very likely, Candidate A's learning curve will be steeper than Candidate B's unless Candidate A's hiring responds to other compelling business needs that obliged the company to hire them based on potential rather than performance. This example is based on our experience: Sleep polysomnography technicians must have a degree in respiratory therapy. However, earning the degree does not make you a sleep polysomnography technician. Therefore, if Candidate A has a degree in respiratory therapy but has never worked in a sleep laboratory, and Candidate B has the degree and worked in a sleep laboratory for five years, the onboarding for Candidate B will be shorter than that for Candidate A.

- **Role complexity.** Straightforward repetitive roles, such as many of those in manufacturing operations, typically require less time to master than roles calling for independent judgment, such as many of those within business planning and forecasting departments.
- **Multiple players.** Typically, an onboarding program will last between a month and a year. As the program's designer, you need to orchestrate the seamless involvement of multiple players over time. These include L&D, HR, company management (including top management), and the employee's manager.

RESOURCES

"Strategic Onboarding: Transforming New Hires Into Dedicated Employees" by Kim Lamoreaux (2008) presents a model where new employee orientation is called a checklist and managed by HR, onboarding is a process managed by the training function, and strategic onboarding is an experience managed by the business function.

The U.S. Army's Acculturation Onboarding Model (2014) takes you through an onboarding program that starts before the first day and takes up to a year. It specifies the responsibilities of the employee and the commander, but can be adapted to nonmilitary settings.

Who Should Undergo Onboarding?

Onboarding allows organizations to facilitate role transitions for employees who are entering another stage within their employee life cycle. At first you may think that these programs should be geared toward those who join your company for the first time. However, new-to-role employees at most levels of the organization should also undergo onboarding; just consider their tenure in the company when deciding in which program components they should participate. For instance, people who have been working for the company between three and five years do not need to attend new employee orientations unless the company has undergone a major change; the same is true for employees at the executive level because they establish business policy and direction. In contrast, those new-to-role employees who have been in the company for more than five years should attend new employee orientations and experience role-specific onboarding, because the circumstances under which they assume their new role vary considerably. The programs that you design for both groups of employees need to consider their similarities and differences. Let's look at these groups and their unique traits.

New Employees

A company's new employees may come from another company in the same industry. For instance, a person who worked in an auto dealership is starting work at another dealership. In this case, the employee's onboarding would emphasize products and customer profiles. Another example would be a university instructor who received an offer to teach at another university; the instructor's onboarding would focus on the university's mission, values, and culture, delving into the particular profile of the department and its students.

In contrast, new employees may have worked in different industries and acquired highly transferable skills over the course of their careers. For instance, an auditor whom you just hired to work at a food and beverages company started in banking, moved to insurance, and then moved to telecommunications. Because the tasks and responsibilities of each of these roles are likely to be similar, at each new job, this person's onboarding experiences will mainly target the applicable rules and regulations for each industry.

Today's workforce is highly mobile, not only nationally, but internationally. Therefore, an employee who had a managerial position in Austria may accept a comparable managerial position in the United States, whether these are in the same or different industries. If the position is in the same industry, then the onboarding would target the similarities and differences between companies, highlighting culture. If, in contrast, the position is in another industry, the new employee would need to spend more time learning about the industry and the position of the business within that industry.

Today's career paths are not as linear as they used to be because organizations have become flatter to become more efficient. Traditionally, when employees received promotions, it was often based on their potential to perform at a different level of responsibility. Although they may have had the potential, they still needed to develop the competencies and skills necessary to perform their new roles and acquire the understanding of how to handle their new responsibilities on an interpersonal level. However, with fewer opportunities for upward mobility, more employees are accepting lateral changes for job enrichment and to prepare them for other positions in the future, whether in the same or another company. In other instances, employees are demoted to a lower-level position because the business needs have changed, their positions have been redefined, or the positions demand a different skill set. Promotions, demotions, and lateral changes can also occur in different countries, which often affords opportunities to broaden an employee's perspective and prepare the individual for the next position somewhere else.

In addition, some employees become known as experts in an industry. Many times, these employees are courted by different companies because of their expertise, often for different roles. For instance, a salesperson may become a sales executive and later an account executive. Then another company offers them a supervisory role, and yet another offers them a managerial opening. In this case, the onboarding has to emphasize knowledge of the company and of the role rather than that of the industry.

Other professionals may hold different positions in different industries. For instance, someone in marketing who started as an analyst for a chocolate manufacturing company can have a senior analyst position at a telecommunications company, move to a supervisory position in software development, and accept another senior analyst position at a news media outlet to gain additional experience. In this case, the employee's onboarding would entail learning about the industry, the company, and the specific role in each move.

New-to-Role Employees

The experience of new to role employees in your company may involve a promotion when an employee is offered and accepts a position of more responsibility, which may or may not entail supervising or managing others to achieve company goals—as is the case of highly technical positions where career progression can be achieved while maintaining status as an individual contributor. For example, a recent graduate with an engineering degree following a technical career path may start as an engineer and later be promoted to senior engineer, principal engineer, and senior principal engineer. In contrast, a recent graduate with an engineering degree following a managerial career path may start as an engineer and later be promoted to senior engineer to then become manager, senior manager, and director.

Demotions occur when an employee, because of performance, business, or development reasons, goes to a position of less or different responsibility. A demotion can be one way to learn about a different function within your company to be ready for another role or to satisfy an employee's temporary or long-term personal need or time commitments.

Lateral changes take place when an employee begins to perform a similar role in another department or function. In this case the employee brings an understanding of the role and general skills and competencies required; however, the employee still needs to become familiar with the department or function and its culture, as well as the subtleties of performing the role within that context.

While deciding which components to include in your onboarding program for new-to-role employees, remember to keep the length of their tenure in the organization in mind. Also, consider if they have executive status when making those decisions (Table 1-1).

Table 1-1. Onboarding Program Components for New-to-Role Employees

New-to-Role Situation	Program Component	
	New Employee Orientation	Role-Specific Onboarding
Promotion	Depends on Tenure and Executive Status	Yes
Demotion	Depends on Tenure and Executive Status	Yes
Lateral Change	Depends on Tenure and Executive Status	Yes
Relocation	Yes	Yes
Perform Work at a Location Different From Where They Report	Yes	Yes
Change in Reporting Location	Yes	Yes
Background in Comparable Role	Depends on Tenure and Executive Status	Yes
New Career Path	Depends on Tenure and Executive Status	Yes

Relocated employees may perform the same role or a different one under conditions of promotions, demotions, or lateral moves; therefore, their onboarding will have to address issues associated with the relocation in addition to those related to the change in responsibility level.

Employees may be working in a location different from where they report when they produce their deliverables. In addition, their supervisors may be assigned to another facility, which could be within or outside the country where the employee is based. In this case, the role-specific onboarding has to address any work-related issues caused by the changing locations, as well as those pertaining to working under these supervisory conditions.

Or perhaps an employee has a background in a comparable role from previous experience at another company. While they were hired to do a different job at your company, they're now going to take a position that resembles the role performed previously. Even though this employee's previous experience in a similar role is valuable, you cannot assume that the role in your company is the same as their previous role because it was at another company, at another time, and under different circumstances. Therefore, you should discuss those differences but without disregarding the value of that history.

New Career Paths

A new career path begins when an employee initiates a different professional trajectory within the company in a new area of the business, either because the employee requested it to explore other options and areas of interest or because the company decided the employee's skill set was a better fit for that area. For example, someone who has held different roles in human resources embarks on a career path in marketing. Regardless of whether the role represents a promotion, demotion, or lateral move, this employee has to master the functional and cultural features of this new career path.

Let's consider the following situation.

Beatrice's Story

Beatrice started in Blanket Corp. as a manufacturing operator. Eager to learn and acquire new skills, she quickly mastered how to use and troubleshoot the equipment in her unit. Even though it was not part of her formal role, Beatrice began to support new employees when they were assigned to her unit. Her supervisors took notice of her leadership skills among her peers and promoted her to supervisor. Because she was such a natural leader, and had been at Blanket Corp. for more than 10 years, no one thought to provide role-specific onboarding for Beatrice. She was left completely on her own to figure out what to do.

Beatrice struggled with the transition as well as the new responsibilities that accompanied her role, such as being a role model for her employees, handling company politics, communicating constantly with her employees and other management levels, and using company systems for transactions related to her new role and employees.

Beatrice made several major mistakes because she did not understand her role or how to interact with her former supervisor. She did not know the difference between exempt and nonexempt employees. She was unable to be a role model for her employees because she continued behaving as an employee instead of as a supervisor. In addition, her emails showed carelessness in thinking as well as writing.

Eleven months into her new role, her manager called her into her office to inform Beatrice of her termination.

Whose responsibility was Beatrice's unsatisfactory performance after a very successful track record as a manufacturing operator?

The company assumed that, because of Beatrice's performance and general skills, she would be able to perform a role that was new for her. Beatrice's example illustrates a common problem in organizations: Promoting an employee to a supervisor without appropriate onboarding or support eventually results in losing the employee, the supervisor, or other employees, and hurting the business.

Although Beatrice was willing and able to assume her new role and had been at Blanket Corp. for more than 10 years, the company where she initiated her career had changed. Thus, like anyone who starts in a new position, she needed to update her knowledge about different aspects of the company, gain a different perspective on it based on her new role, and obtain the necessary information to succeed. For all practical purposes, Beatrice, like any other employee who assumes a supervisory or managerial position, was a new employee who needed to receive role-specific onboarding.

Let's meet Ramiah.

Ramiah's Story

Ramiah was a marketing manager at a waste management company. When the company decided to outsource the marketing function as a cost-reduction measure, she was offered a position as accounts payable analyst because of her background in accounting. This change represented a significant demotion for Ramiah; however, it was a better option for her than sudden unemployment. She agreed to stay.

When Ramiah's manager explained the business situation that led to the outsourcing decision, he allowed her to ask questions and granted her a week's leave to prepare for her new role. Meanwhile, her previous manager held several meetings with her peers and direct reports, communicating Ramiah's change in role and position and emphasizing how her background in accounting would allow her to contribute to the business.

When she returned from her leave, Ramiah found that her new supervisor had already planned an individualized onboarding program for her to learn about her new role and move forward. This was a very important step in her transition.

Ramiah was engaged and believed that she was set for success.

Beatrice's and Ramiah's companies handled their shifts into their new roles in totally different ways. Beatrice's company did not offer role-specific onboarding, while Ramiah's did. The combination of personal and company factors involved in these experiences led to completely different results.

Today's career paths are anything but linear—as organizations continue to flatten, career paths go upward, downward, and sideways. It is not uncommon for someone to take a lateral assignment or even a position that is one or more levels below their current one to gain valuable experience before their next move. Ramiah's example stretches our thinking about the need for onboarding beyond external hires or promotions. Her change in role demanded an individualized onboarding program just as much as anyone else's role transition. Although Ramiah's change is considered a step backward by many, it allowed her to use her background in a different way and remain with an organization where she enjoyed working. The way in which Ramiah's onboarding was handled allowed her to see this change as a temporary step from which to continue moving forward.

Other groups of employees who need to undergo onboarding are those who are relocating within a company in their home country or abroad.

Dimitri's Story

Dimitri is the senior analyst at Mikka's and has been with the company for eight years. He recently learned that he is considered a high-potential employee, and his individualized development plan includes a transfer to the company's new office in Lima, Peru. To his advantage, Dimitri is fully bilingual.

Even though Dimitri's change entails a lateral move within the s[...] he will be new to the role and to the company's operations in Lir[...] of the company's size and the frequency of this type of assignme[...] has an onboarding program that begins before its employees ar[...] new assignment. The program includes a wide range of informa[...] company's operations in Lima, with plenty of opportunities to a[...] connect with other employees before arriving to increase the likelihood of success.

After his manager announced his transfer to the Lima office, Dimitri visited the new office in Lima for onboarding several times before assuming his position. He received and read the company's country-specific employee handbook, met his peers and future team, and got a hands-on understanding of the culture of the company at that location as well as of the location itself. With the support of a local mentor, he learned about the business, office jargon, what to say, and what not to say, as well as how to handle radically different perceptions of time. By the time Dimitri started in his new role, he was ready to perform. He understood the role and the culture.

Dimitri's example illustrates an onboarding program that started several months before his role changed and required the involvement of multiple players over time. It reinforces how onboarding, like many other employee experiences, calls for the careful orchestration of the efforts of experts, facilitators, supporters, and stakeholders whose job is to ease that important transition for business success.

Stakeholders of Employee Onboarding

Employee onboarding requires full responsibility from learning and development with the joint support of human resources, management, department heads, other employees, peers, and direct reports to deliver the employee value proposition that attracted candidates to the company in the first place. The manager enables the general and role-specific onboarding processes, and the new or new-to-role employee co-creates the onboarding process as an active participant in this stage of their career.

As you review their roles and responsibilities, consider preparing a matrix of all the activities and the decision-making authority associated with them in the form of a RACI chart (Responsible, Accountable, Consulted, and Informed). Such a chart will give you and the company a visual portrayal that will prove useful for rebalancing and reassigning responsibilities and tasks throughout your onboarding program.

Stakeholder role clarification in onboarding will pay off throughout the program's design and implementation, minimizing confusion and maintaining that positive impression on the new or the new-to-role employee. In turn, program participants

...nefit from the right combination of resources, expertise, and tenure brought to the table for them. Onboarding is one of the business's best practices for employees, managers, and executives.

TOOL

The "RACI Chart Sample and Template" located at the end of this chapter is useful to visualize how the responsibilities and decision-making authority are distributed in your onboarding program.

Understanding the Big Picture

General onboarding addresses big-picture company topics. Role-specific onboarding tackles role definition in detail. Onboarding cuts across organizational levels with the involvement of multiple stakeholders along the way. How you handle relationships with those different stakeholders will influence the results of your program.

In the next chapter we will guide you through the many benefits of onboarding as a preparation for understanding your own program needs.

Questions to Explore

- How does your organization define onboarding?
- Why is onboarding important to your organization?
- Who are the stakeholders of your onboarding program?
- Does your organization differentiate between employee orientation and employee onboarding?
- What is your company doing to ease the transition of new employees into the company's culture?
- What is the company doing to assist employees as they assume new roles and perform their new functions?
- What does the company do between the moment when new employees accept the employment offer and their first day?

- How does the company handle any differences in background during onboarding?
- How does the company address specific issues related to promotions, demotions, lateral moves, or transfers among employees who are assuming new roles during onboarding?

Tools for Support

Pre-Onboarding Checklist

Use this checklist to ensure completion of all pre-onboarding tasks.

Employee Name:				
Department:		Position:		
Manager's Name:		Start Date:		
Completed by:		Date:		

Item	Status			
	Not Completed	In Progress	Completed	Comments
1. Review employee's application to get acquainted with background				
2. Review job description for tasks and responsibilities				
3. Prepare customized orientation materials and documents				
4. Review onboarding schedule				
5. Verify accurate completion of documents, including signatures and dates				
6. Confirm that the following documents (if applicable by industry or position) are on file:				
a. Background check				
b. Reference check				
c. Form I-9				
d. Tax withholding forms				

Item	Status			
	Not Completed	In Progress	Completed	Comments
e. Drug screening results				
f. Emergency contact information				
g. Direct deposit authorization for payroll				
h. Benefits' enrollment				
i. Credit references				
j. Driving record				
k. Immunizations				
l. Noncompetition agreement				
m. Security information				
n. Employment at will				
7. Inform all relevant stakeholders of employee's arrival				

RACI Chart Sample and Template

Use this chart to help you visualize how the responsibilities and decision-making authority are distributed in your onboarding program. Review the sample chart and then use the template to analyze your own program.

Definitions:
- Responsible (R): who completes the work
- Accountable (A): who is ultimately accountable or who can say yes or no about the work
- Consulted (C): who gives feedback and contributes to the work
- Informed (I): who needs to know

Sample RACI Chart

Activities	Responsible (R)	Accountable (A)	Consulted (C)	Informed (I)
Collect exit interview data	Janice	Helen	Irwing	Layla
Analyze exit interview data	Janice	Helen	Frederika	
Report results of exit interview data	Janice	Helen	Frederika	Héctor
Identify key issues related to onboarding program	Helen	Helen		Alberto
Revisit onboarding program to address issues raised	Héctor	Alberto		

Analysis

What are the data telling you? Look at the patterns. If someone has several Rs, this may not be realistic. If someone seems to be making every decision, these may be delayed. If several individuals need to be consulted about everything, question if their input is really necessary. Evaluate who needs to be informed, when, and how.

Use this blank chart to do your own **RACI** analysis.

RACI Analysis Template

Activities	Responsible (R)	Accountable (A)	Consulted (C)	Informed (I)

Additional Resources

Chao, G.T. 2012. "Organizational Socialization: Background, Basics, and Blueprint for Adjustment at Work." Chapter 18 in *The Oxford Handbook of Organizational Psychology*, vol. 1, edited by S.W.J. Kozlowski. New York: Oxford University Press.

Crebar, A. 2018. "Top 7 Employee Onboarding Programs." Sapling HR, April 15. www.saplinghr.com/blog/top-7-employee-onboarding-programs.

Derven, M. 2008. "Management Onboarding: Obtain Early Allegiance to Gain a Strategic Advantage in the War for Talent." *T+D*, April: 49-52.

Hampel, B., and E. Lamont. 2011. *Perfect Phrases for New Employee Orientation and Onboarding.* New York: McGraw Hill.

Lamoreaux, K. 2008. "Strategic Onboarding: Transforming New Hires Into Dedicated Employees." *Bersin and Associates Research Bulletin* 3:1. http://mms.gpstrategies.com /pdf/010408_RB_Onboarding_KL_Final.pdf.

Ritz-Carlton Leadership Center. 2015. "Culture and Onboarding." Ritz-Carlton blog, December 2. http://ritzcarltonleadershipcenter.com/2015/12/culture-and -onboarding.

Sims, D.M. 2011. *Creative Onboarding Programs: Tools for Energizing Your Orientation Programs.* New York: McGraw Hill.

Tynan, K. 2010. *Survive Your Promotion: The 90 Day Success Plan for New Managers.* Hudson, MA: Personal Focus Press.

U.S. Army. 2014. *United States Army Civilian Acculturation Program Handbook.* www.tradoc .army.mil/dcspil/acculturation/documents/AcculturationHandbook.pdf.

Vernon, A. 2012. *90 Days 90 Ways: Onboard Young Professionals to Peak Performance.* Alexandria, VA: ASTD Press.

Wesson, M.J., and C.I. Gogus. 2005. "Shaking Hands With a Computer: An Examination of Two Methods of Organizational Newcomer Orientation." *Journal of Applied Psychology* 90(5): 1018-26.

2

Shaping the Future: Why Start an Onboarding Program?

In This Chapter

- General benefits of an onboarding program
- Benefits for the business
- Benefits for managers
- Benefits for employees
- When onboarding fails and why

Understanding the Benefits of Onboarding

Consider the following facts:

- "A full one third of external hires are not with the organization after two years. . . . Less than one third of executives worldwide are positive about their onboarding experience. . . . Almost one third of executives who joined organizations as an external hire miss expectations in the first two years. . . . Almost one third of employees employed in their current job for less than six months are already job searching" (Morgan 2017).

- "Formal onboarding increases the chance of keeping a new employee for at least three years by 69 percent" (Lombardi and Laurano 2013).

- "Only one half of new hires rated their onboarding programs highly" (Boatman and Erker 2012).

- "According to a study from Equifax, more than half of all employees who left their job in the past year did so within the first 12 months" (Forbes 2017).

Onboarding affects business results, and when it goes wrong, it means time and financial losses. These include company investments in recruitment and selection as well as initial L&D efforts. For example, on average, companies invest between $4,000 for a frontline employee and $50,000 or more for an executive for recruitment and selection, including:

- identifying and defining the need for the job
- revising the job description
- creating and announcing the job posting
- receiving, monitoring, and screening resumes
- preparing interview questions and interviewers
- scheduling and conducting interviews
- selecting candidates
- administering assessments (if applicable)
- negotiating employee contracts
- completing background checks
- tailoring benefits
- completing paperwork.

In some instances, the company may have to add travel expenses to interview candidates as well as relocation costs if these are part of the employment offer. In addition, many companies secure the services of external headhunting services to hire executives, which represents additional costs.

TOOL

The "Recruitment and Selection Task Checklist," located at the end of this chapter, is useful for verifying that all recruitment and selection tasks are completed before the new employee arrives.

Unfortunately, many organizations underestimate the value and benefits that a solid onboarding program provides for the business, managers, and employees regardless of level. However, other companies invest significantly in onboarding programs. For example:

- Kimberly-Clark's website introduces potential candidates to its People Philosophy (welcome, dream, grow, win, celebrate, live well, and give back) so they can explore how to "unleash their power" at the company. The website also explains the entire application process and includes useful resources, such as tips for resumes and social media as well as on-site, telephone, and video interviewing. Upon hiring, new employees have access to another password-protected website that streamlines the onboarding process by allowing them to complete paperwork before their first day.

- At Zappos, regardless of role, new hires participate in four weeks of customer service training. This introduces them to the entire process of handling customers. After the first three weeks of training, Zappos extends "The Offer" to anyone who does not consider themselves a good fit for the company. This payout, which fluctuates between $2,000 and $4,000, becomes the last screening mechanism for selecting employees who are best suited for the business before incurring any additional costs.

- At Cleveland Clinic, the video "Empathy Series: The Human Connection to Patient Care" is used to show how the hospital establishes connections between patients and staff. It is often used as a tool to promote interest in working at the clinic. "The Cleveland Clinic Orientation Welcome" video highlights the organization's culture of caregiving and the high standards to which new employees are accountable. It's one of many resources designed for employees across career paths to support their development and growth.

Effective employee onboarding programs set the foundation for employee engagement beyond those first months we typically call "the honeymoon period," where the employee is figuring out what to do and what to avoid doing in the new workplace. Employees who undergo onboarding programs typically express higher levels of engagement with their companies and their positions because they feel valued and supported. They understand their employer's value proposition and brand because they can see the connection between what the company says and what it stands for. Employee onboarding programs allow organizations to strengthen their brand and attract top talent capable of assuming other roles in the future as part of the company's succession planning process. The benefits of onboarding extend to the business, managers, and employees.

Benefits to the Business

Employees feel welcomed and valued when companies offer onboarding programs, which typically results in lower turnover rates. Less turnover, in turn, leads to considerable cost savings in recruiting, selecting, and training new employees; workforce stability also reduces productivity losses.

Employees are less likely to miss work when they master what they do. Onboarding can ensure a strong cultural fit, which also translates into lower absenteeism rates. Thus, the organization can expect with a higher degree of certainty that its workforce will be available to complete the work without having to incur overtime costs to cover its needs on short notice or to resort to contingency employees on a long-term basis. In addition to increased costs, companies have to consider the effects of physical and mental fatigue on employees who work overtime, particularly over extended periods, and the subsequent risks of such practice.

A reputation for solid onboarding programs becomes a competitive advantage for top talent because such companies are attractive for employees who want to advance in their careers and have options for global mobility and technology-enhanced opportunities for job flexibility. Through their onboarding programs, companies demonstrate that they are willing to invest in the development of their employees and their success from the moment of hiring. Top candidates who can choose where they work and how they work are more willing to seriously consider what these companies have to offer. Therefore, the overall qualifications of the candidate pool become more solid, which converts into a better qualified and more competitive workforce to achieve business results.

Valuable relationships begin to be established during participation in company onboarding programs. Employees gain a deeper understanding of the company culture and can identify who will be able to support them as well as whom they will need to support in given situations. Higher levels of collaboration and communication between employees and across the organization are often a consequence of those initial contacts. The time that it takes newcomers to be accepted and integrated into the company's culture shortens because those interactions foster familiarity.

RESOURCE

In *The 2020 Workplace: How Innovative Companies Attract, Develop, and Keep Tomorrow's Employees Today*, Jeanne C. Meister and Karie Willyerd (2010) offer projections about workplace trends that can help you develop practices fitting today's technological world.

An up-front investment in an employee's onboarding, particularly in the role-specific component, leads to higher levels of productivity in a shorter amount of time. An employee with proper onboarding starts beating the learning curve at a faster pace from the first day on the job than one without.

Onboarding programs that convey consistent messages about the company's brand allow employees to identify with the brand, internalize it, and promote it among internal and external clients. As the company's brand comes alive for employees, that positive first impression leads employees to form a stronger bond with the company itself. Subsequent company brand reinforcement generates a spiraling effect that, in turn, serves to attract clients and job candidates.

RESOURCE

The video "An Insider Look at Microsoft HK MACH Program for Graduates" includes many testimonials about Microsoft's academy and its impact. It highlights the importance of building a culture of collaboration that leverages multiple diverse development opportunities and technology to empower and support its employees.

Onboarding also allows organizations to address policies, laws, and regulations about harassment, domestic violence, equal employment opportunities, and occupational health and safety through a single voice that becomes a mechanism for proactive risk management. When companies spend time discussing these issues instead of simply relying on employees reading and interpreting those documents on their own, not only do they convey the information consistently to all new employees, but they also show that these issues are important.

An employee's sense of emotional connection with the business increases as a result of gaining another perspective about the organization and its culture through a company's onboarding program. As employees begin to understand how they can contribute to the success of the business, their level of engagement increases. Higher levels of employee engagement are consistently associated with higher revenues and profitability. In the words of industry leader Ken Oehler, global culture and engagement practice leader at Aon

PRO TIP

Provide new employees with a firsthand glimpse of what it is like to work at your company by enlisting current employees to share their experiences.

Hewitt (2017): "Improving engagement can pay dividends: a five point increase in employee engagement is linked to a three point increase in revenue growth the following year."

Further, Gallup's *State of the American Workplace* report for 2015-2016 states that "disengaged employees cost the country somewhere between $450B and $550B each year." Thus, investments in employee onboarding become investments in employee engagement.

RESOURCE

Brian Baker and Brad Warga (2010), in "Building Excitement for Opening Day: A Case Study on New Employee Engagement at Harrah's Entertainment," describe how Harrah's changed its onboarding program into one that would lead participants to understand their cultural fit and improve business metrics instead of only developing skills.

Feedback from new employees during onboarding programs gives organizations information about what they need to address to be more effective to satisfy their emerging talent needs. This unique opportunity to retrofit the company's recruitment, selection, and onboarding processes delivers competitive advantages by allowing companies to anticipate the needs of its current and future workforces. They can use this information to design mechanisms that address those needs before the competition does, thus increasing the prospects of having more qualified candidates for positions and reducing the likelihood of new employee turnover and its associated costs.

When employment is stable, HR staff can spend more time addressing business-related workforce issues than completing transactions and paperwork. Likewise, management can focus on running the business with the right people in the right place, instead of constantly worrying about replacements, handling disciplinary issues related to attendance and productivity, and meeting short-term business needs.

Benefits to Managers

Onboarding is designed to initiate and foster contact between employees and their managers from the start, thus encouraging communication. Open and honest communication between managers and employees is important because it's how managers convey important business information, control the work that is done, and motivate employees to complete tasks. Communication further influences the outcomes of the employee-manager relationship, especially when managers can identify the best way to share information with every employee.

The beginning of the employee-manager relationship during onboarding is the best time for them to determine what to expect from one another. Role-specific onboarding grants multiple opportunities for managers to interact with their employees, get to know them, clarify roles, and align expectations. Managers can optimize the time spent in individual meetings, on-the-job training, and department orientations, as well as setting up coffee and meal breaks to get to know employees. Time invested at the beginning of the relationship leads to better understanding of what the manager and the employee need from one another, as well as what each will give and receive. Clearer definition of role boundaries and greater time spent producing results are also outcomes of this initial stage of the relationship. In addition, managers can spell out individual and team responsibilities at the department or unit levels, reinforcing how tasks are distributed across the team and thus promoting team efforts when these are relevant.

Through planned and unplanned interactions that are part of onboarding, employees and managers learn to trust one another as they get to know one another. Trust is a fundamental component of the employee-manager relationship that transcends the boundaries of everyday interactions and often accounts for that extra discretionary effort from an employee that translates into higher performance, productivity, loyalty, and engagement. Moreover, trust contributes to creating a safe work environment where managers and employees can take risks and innovate, knowing that they can rely on one another.

RESOURCE

Stephen Covey (2006) provides the foundations for leaders to create a culture of trust in *The Speed of Trust: The One Thing That Changes Everything*. The book takes readers through five waves (self, relationships, organizational, market, and societal) that make establishing trust actionable.

Benefits to Employees

Employees meet key individuals within and outside their own departments or units with whom they will interact throughout their careers during general and role-specific onboarding programs. These interactions go beyond traditional presentations of ever-changing organizational charts, and contribute to building valuable relationships that will facilitate their work in their new roles. These relationships may take additional meanings later on, as employees start to consider different career options within and outside the organization. For instance, peers from the same department can share information about dos and don'ts in the workplace, peers from other departments can provide insights on how other areas of the business are run, and supervisors and managers can become formal or informal mentors.

As employees participate in onboarding programs, they learn what to do and when to do it, thus requiring less support and increasing their own sense of self-efficacy and self-assurance on the job. Employees who are comfortable within the culture of their companies and their departments become effective business contributors and demonstrate higher levels of satisfaction with their positions and companies. When employees are satisfied with their jobs, they are more likely to stay.

As employees learn more about the company, where it has been, and where it is going, as well as experience what it is like to work there, they establish a robust link with the organization. A stronger connection with the business gives employees a sense of career stability because they see themselves as part of the present and future of the company. They can also visualize their career path in the company, thus their commitment to the workplace increases.

Open discussions about company culture and realistic job previews, even before the selection process is complete, allow potential employees to make better choices about where they want to work, based on their own experiences and preferences. These discussions let candidates make informed decisions when they receive an employment offer and later confirm that they made the right choice because they fit well with the company's culture. Therefore, any impulse to quit after the first setback diminishes significantly.

RESOURCE

The 2016 Deloitte report *The New Organizations: Different by Design* challenges onboarding program designers to stay up-to-date on workforce trends.

The bonds employees build during onboarding with their managers and peers also provide a support system that reduces stress and anxiety levels related to their new roles. When employees know that they can count on a strong support system of professionals who know what it is like to work in the company and can offer valuable advice to handle different situations based on lessons learned, they are more capable of focusing their energies on the tasks at hand and succeed at them.

If Onboarding Fails

Like many other company programs and initiatives, onboarding programs don't always deliver the expected results. It is the L&D function's responsibility to identify the cause if the program fails.

Given onboarding's significance, a successful program is essential. As you think about your own company's onboarding program, you want to avoid any potential pitfalls that could make it unsuccessful. Even though onboarding programs typically fail because of insufficient planning, time, and resources, there are other not so obvious reasons that can make a difference in the outcome of your program, including:

- onboarding and reality don't match
- lack of employee engagement with the onboarding program
- no compelling business case for the onboarding program
- lack of sense of belonging or recognition, especially if the employee is left to have lunch alone
- employee misfit with the company

RESOURCE

Talya N. Bauer's 2010 report *Onboarding New Employees: Maximizing Success* introduces trends and prospective tendencies in onboarding programs that are valuable for program designers who want to prepare their organizations for the workforce of the future.

- ignoring diverse needs, metrics, and accountability
- a "do it yourself" mentality, where no one assumes responsibility or ownership for onboarding
- programs that focus only on employee benefits
- unavailability, lack of involvement, and lack of guidance from managers
- information overload at a high-speed pace
- misconstruing onboarding as a checklist or time to complete orientation paperwork
- skipping definition and discussion of company expectations, and delaying explanations about how the employee will contribute to the business
- assuming new employees will understand how their role fits within the organization without providing detailed information
- assuming unwritten rules are self-evident
- believing that a full agenda of activities and events for the employee to meet key people depending on the role is unnecessary
- explaining how performance will be evaluated at the time of reviews
- expecting employees to perform the role on their own without giving enough time to develop a basic level of role mastery.

TOOL

Use the "Onboarding Program Audit Checklist" located at the end of this chapter to audit your program and avoid any pitfalls on your way to success.

Being Proactive for Success

Onboarding is a process that demands a thorough understanding. By knowing its benefits, you will gain full ownership of the program. Onboarding is the first step in the employee's life cycle, whether they are new to the company or to the role. Because failing in onboarding is not an option, you need to take a proactive stance to make the program a success.

In the next chapter we will guide you through the five phases to design your onboarding program.

Questions to Explore

- How much does your company invest every time a new employee joins the organization?
- When calculating the investment in a new employee, which tasks does your company include? For instance, does it include the salaries of HR staff and costs of printing materials?
- What are the most important benefits of onboarding for the business that your company has identified?
- Has your company acknowledged that onboarding programs have benefits for managers? If so, what are some examples?
- Has your company considered the potential benefits of onboarding programs for employees? If so, what are some examples?
- Have any previous onboarding efforts not produced the expected results? If so, what did your company do?
- What will you tell your company's management and leaders about the benefits of onboarding?

Tools for Support

Recruitment and Selection Task Checklist

Use the results of this tool to identify which tasks still need to be completed before the new employee's arrival.

Employee Name:				
Department:	Position:			
Manager's Name:	Start Date:			
Completed by:	Date:			
Item	Status			
	Not Completed	In Progress	Completed	Comments
1. Identify and define need for job				
2. Revise job description				
3. Create and announce job posting				
4. Receive, monitor, and screen resumes				
5. Prepare interview questions and interviewers				
6. Schedule and conduct interviews				
7. Select candidates				
8. Administer assessments (if applicable)				
9. Negotiate employee contract				
10. Complete background checks				
11. Tailor benefits				
12. Complete paperwork				

Onboarding Program Audit Checklist

Use this checklist to audit your onboarding program and avoid a,
way to success. The items that you check as "no" will point you to factors ,
address to avoid failure. Turn them into action items to strengthen your program.

Program Component:			
Completed by:	Date:		
Factor	Status		
	Yes	No	Comments
Onboarding and workplace reality match			
Employees are engaged with onboarding program			
Full guidance from managers for employees			
Compelling business case			
Recognition for program			
Good employee cultural fit			
Availability of metrics or accountability			
Acknowledgment of diverse needs			
Program focus beyond employee benefits			
Availability and involvement of managers			
Clarity in who is responsible for onboarding			
Quantity of information is appropriate to avoid overload			
Information is delivered at pace conducive to comprehension			
Onboarding is not seen as a checklist or time to complete orientation paperwork			
Company expectations about the role are defined and described			
Provides detailed information about how the employee's role fits within the organization			
Gives high priority to explaining how the employee will contribute to the business in the role			
Attention to reaching out to meet the new employee			
Assumes that unwritten rules are not self-evident			

	Yes	No	Comments
Includes a full agenda of activities and events for the employee to meet key people depending on the role			
Ensures that someone takes the new employee to lunch			
Explains how performance will be evaluated upon assuming role			
Gives employee enough time to develop a basic level of role mastery before expecting them to perform it			
Maximizes the amount of paperwork that must be completed before the employee's arrival			

Additional Resources

Aon Hewitt. 2017. *2017 Trends in Global Employee Engagement: Global Anxiety Erodes Employee Engagement Gains.* www.aon.com/engagement17.

Baker, B., and B. Warga. 2010. "Building Excitement for Opening Day: A Case Study on New Employee Engagement at Harrah's Entertainment." Aon Hewitt. www.aon.com/attachments/harrahs.pdf.

Bauer, T.N. 2010. *Onboarding New Employees: Maximizing Success.* Alexandria, VA: Society for Human Resources Management Foundation.

Boatman, J., and S. Erker. 2012. *Global Selection Forecast 2012.* Development Dimensions International. www.ddiworld.com/DDI/media/trend-research/globalselection forecast2012_tr_ddi.pdf?ext=.pdf.

Bradt, G., and M. Vonnegut. 2009. *Onboarding: How to Get Your New Employees Up to Speed in Half the Time.* Hoboken, NJ: John Wiley & Sons.

Carmody, K. 2017. "7 Ways to Measure the Effectiveness of an Onboarding Program." SilkRoad, August 30. www.silkroad.com/blog/7-ways-measure-effectiveness -onboarding-program.

Cheng, A. 2017. "On Holacracy, Customer Service, and 'Zappos Anything.'" eMarketer Retail, April 7. https://retail.emarketer.com/article/zappos-ceo-tony-hsieh-on -holacracy-customer-service-zappos-anything/58e8084eebd4000a54864afc.

Cleveland Clinic. 2013. "Empathy: The Human Connection to Patient Care." Cleveland Clinic's Empathy Series, February 27. www.youtube.com/watch?v=cDDWvj_q-o8.

Cooper, B.B. 2018. "Onboarding Best Practices: How the Smartest Companies Turn New Hires Into Great Employees." Foundr, May 3. https://foundr.com /onboarding-best-practices.

Covey, S.M.R. 2006. *The Speed of Trust: The One Thing That Changes Everything.* With R.R. Merrill. New York: Free Press.

Deloitte. 2016. *Global Human Capital Trends 2016.* "The New Organizations: Different by Design." Deloitte University Press. www2.deloitte.com/content/dam/Deloitte /global/Documents/HumanCapital/gx-dup-global-human-capital-trends-2016.pdf.

Forbes Coaches Council. 2017. "Seven New Onboarding Strategies You'll See This Year." Forbes Community Voice, January 30. www.forbes.com/sites/forbescoachescouncil /2017/01/30/seven-new-onboarding-strategies-youll-see-this-year/#1b9f3f387b4d.

Gallup. 2017. "State of the American Workplace." https://news.gallup.com/reports /199961/state-american-workplace-report-2017.aspx.

HCI (Human Capital Institute). 2016. "The Unrecognized Potential of Onboarding and Offboarding: Getting the Most of the On-demand Economy." HCI, May 19. www.hci.org/hr-research/unrecognized-potential-and-boarding-getting-most-out -ondemand-economy.

Kimberly Clark. n.d. "Careers." www.careersatkc.com.

L'Oreal Talent. n.d. "Careers at L'Oreal." https://careers2.loreal.com.

Lombardi, M., and M. Laurano. 2013. *Human Capital Management Trends 2013: It's a Brave New World.* Aberdeen Group. www.aberdeen.com/assets/report-preview /8101-RA-human-capital-management.pdf.

Meister, J.C., and K. Willyerd. 2010. *The 2020 Workplace: How Innovative Companies Attract, Develop, and Keep Tomorrow's Employees Today.* New York: Harper Business.

Microsoft HK. 2016. "An Insider Look at Microsoft HK MACH Program for Graduates." September 8. www.youtube.com/watch?v=KoW5FjtUrYU.

Morgan, J. 2017. *The Employee Experience Advantage.* Hoboken, NJ: John Wiley & Sons.

PwC. 2016. *The Future of Onboarding.* December. www.pwc.com/il/he/bankim/assets /pwc-the-future-of-onboarding.pdf.

Sims, D.M. 2011. *Creative Onboarding Programs: Tools for Energizing Your Orientation Programs.* New York: McGraw-Hill.

Stein, M.A., and L. Christiansen. 2010. *Successful Onboarding: A Strategy to Unlock Hidden Value Within Your Organization.* New York: McGraw-Hill.

WeareDNA. n.d. "Onboarding Website: Kimberly Clark." Our DNA Case Studies. www.wearedna.co.uk/case-studies/onboarding-website-kimberly-clark.

Zappos Insights. 2018. "Sharing the Zappos Culture With the World." www.zappos insight.com.

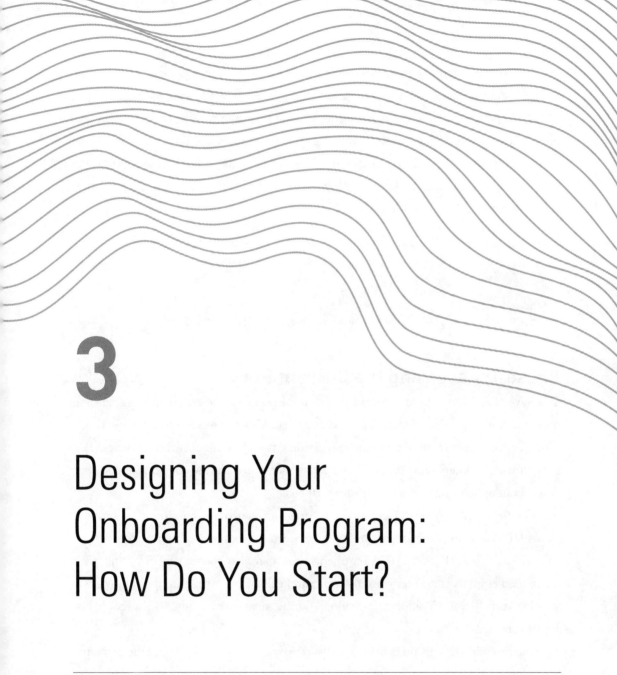

3

Designing Your Onboarding Program: How Do You Start?

In This Chapter

- Understanding your onboarding program's current state
- Defining your onboarding program's desired state
- Completing a gap analysis
- Building and getting approval for your business case

Your onboarding program's design will encompass five phases: assessing the current state, defining the desired state, analyzing the gap, closing the gap, and building the business case for onboarding (Figure 3-1). In this chapter we discuss how to approach each phase with concrete steps that will guide you to obtain the information you will need to design and deliver an effective onboarding program. We begin with what you need to do to establish your program's starting point, based on what the company has done so far about employee onboarding.

Figure 3-1. The Five Phases of Designing an Onboarding Program

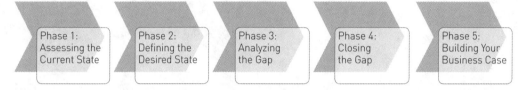

| Phase 1: Assessing the Current State | Phase 2: Defining the Desired State | Phase 3: Analyzing the Gap | Phase 4: Closing the Gap | Phase 5: Building Your Business Case |

Phase 1: Assessing the Current State

You have been charged with designing and implementing the company's onboarding program. You have a lot of ideas about what you could do; however, you know that such an endeavor requires careful planning and dividing tasks into manageable activities. The stakes are high. Where do you start? You need to ascertain what the company already has done about onboarding before you move further.

The first step is to look at the company program's current state from the points of view of the business and its employees. Your primary sources of information will be your company's L&D and HR departments. You can also conduct focus groups with onboarded employees and onboarding program facilitators. We encourage you to interview between 10 and 15 different individuals during separate meetings, which should last approximately 90 minutes.

The first and perhaps most obvious question you need to ask is whether the company has an onboarding program in place or had one recently. The answer will direct the path you follow to obtain the rest of the information you need about the current state (Figure 3-2).

For example, if the company has an onboarding program, you can revise it, revamp it, or transform it into a new onboarding program. In contrast, if the company does not have an onboarding program, your responsibility will be to find out what, if anything, the company is doing to ease the transition of employees into the workplace.

Let's take each path separately and consider the information that asking each question will provide.

Figure 3-2. Paths to Assess Current State of Onboarding Program

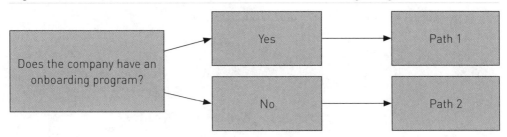

Path 1: The Company Has an Onboarding Program in Place

Revising company onboarding and new employee orientation programs every year is a best practice. When was the last time the company's programs were revised and updated?

If the answer is more than three years, the business has likely undergone significant changes since the last iteration was developed. The reasons that prompted the program revision can give insights into the organization's culture and business needs. If politics played a role, the company probably revised the program because of a change in

TOOL

If your company already has an onboarding program in place, use the "Interview Guide to Define the Current State if the Company Has an Onboarding Program" at the end of this chapter.

management, culture, mission, or vision. A mandate from a regulatory agency or law could also prompt program revisions. Identifying what changed will help you track the program's trajectory and give you some glimpses into future changes.

What is the company's vision for the onboarding program?

Understanding how the company sees the onboarding program is a good starting point to explore its current state. This will be useful as you gather additional information about what the company is doing and the results the program is obtaining. For example, the results may or may not be aligned with the company's vision.

What does the company want to achieve with this program?

There is a relationship between the company's vision for the program, what specific needs the program should address, and what the company wants the program to achieve, which in turn has to be translated into the program's goal.

To illustrate what you will need to do to define program goals, see the sidebar, which provides a snapshot of the Wuud Home Center.

Company Profile for Wuud Home Center

Vision: To be the supplier of choice for home remodeling projects with the best prices, products, and services through the best employees.

History: Wuud Home Center was founded in 1975 as a family business. Today, it is a conglomerate with stores across the northeast coast of the United States, concentrated in Massachusetts and Maine. Wuud firmly believes that its employees are its most important asset.

Current Situation: 14 percent turnover rate among forklift drivers, or approximately 420 forklift drivers per year.

Number of Employees: 3,000.

Target Population: Forklift drivers.

Results of Exit Interviews: Only 23 have been completed, but most exiting personnel mentioned that company promises were not met, there was a disconnect between what employees were expected to do and had to do, and their role was simply not what they expected. Many were disappointed because what they heard during orientation and the reality that they faced when they started to work were unrelated.

Engagement Survey Scores: Below 65 percent.

Performance Evaluations: Inconsistencies and lack of information are the trend.

Additional Information: Onboarding has been an issue for Wuud Home Center because of time constraints. For the past two years, they have only given a half-day orientation using a dated video, followed by three days of role-specific training. New employees pick up their real role responsibilities day by day. Managers believe that they have too much to do, so employees should "start yesterday." If someone is hired, they should know what to do and start doing it upon arrival.

Company Concern: HR and top management are worried about the increasing costs of turnover and the impact on the bottom line.

Proposed Goal: A role-specific onboarding program for forklift drivers.

Did Wuud Home Center express the organization's expectation for the program in a way that makes it possible to achieve it? To find out, let's apply the SMART criteria to its goal to see if it is achievable:

- (S) Is it specific? Does it spell out what needs to be done unambiguously?
- (M) Is it measurable? Does it allow the organization to see its progress toward achieving it in quantifiable terms, especially as it relates to business results?

- (A) Is it actionable? Does it require that something be done?
- (R) Is it realistic? Is the challenge directly proportional to the capacity to achieve it?
- (T) Is it time bound? Assigning a time limit focuses efforts on what needs to be done and makes it easier to measure milestones along the way.

According to the SMART criteria, the goal of creating a role-specific onboarding program for forklift drivers is not specific enough, and it is unclear how the company will measure it. Although it includes elements that are actionable, the goal could bring about unexpected results because it allows for multiple interpretations about how to take action to achieve it. Further, it is not realistic for a company to quickly turn a half-day, general new employee orientation program into a full-fledged differentiated onboarding program. Therefore, the potential costs of not being able to establish the program could be higher than maintaining the status quo. Finally, the timeline for when the company expects to have the program in place is vague.

Based on the SMART criteria, the company's goals should be to:

- Complete a full organizational snapshot for Wuud Home Center to determine the onboarding program's current state and define its desired state.
- Design an onboarding program for forklift drivers that bridges the gap found through the organizational snapshot by the end of the third quarter.

Drafting the goal in alignment with the SMART criteria establishes a guidepost for the gap analysis.

What does the company do to welcome and ease the transition of new employees into the organization?

Find out what the company does, whether it's activities, training sessions, meetings, or something else. The common tendency is to mischaracterize new employee orientations as onboarding programs. For example, someone may tell you that the company has an onboarding program, when it is actually only giving out a welcome packet to employees. Ask for specific examples of what is done to ensure the onboarding program really exists.

Who is the current owner of the employee onboarding program?

Typically, L&D and HR either separately or jointly own employee onboarding programs. In smaller businesses, the owner or the general manager may conduct onboarding. In other cases, onboarding just happens. A lack of clear ownership results in a lack of accountability.

Who are the program stakeholders?

The snapshot of the onboarding program's current state must identify the program's stakeholders. They enter and exit the process multiple times, so knowing who they are helps you find out how they prepare to participate. Potential stakeholders include boards of directors, business owners, HR, operations, and quality.

How are recruitment and selection involved in the onboarding program?

Many books consider onboarding only within the context of recruitment and selection. We believe that recruitment and selection play an important role in employee onboarding because onboarding begins with the business decision to open a position. However, recruitment and selection represent the first two of many elements of an onboarding program that are part of the pre-onboarding phase introduced in chapter 1.

Is the onboarding program designed only for new employees or does it also include current employees and transfers who are assuming new roles?

Companies often only focus their onboarding efforts on external hires, based on the assumption that they need to obtain a general understanding of the new organization. Even though this is true, current employees or transfers who are assuming new roles also need to undergo onboarding when they transfer or when their roles change. As mentioned in chapter 1, the time that has elapsed since the employees' roles changed and whether they are at an executive level will determine their needs.

PRO TIP

Establish priorities for information based on its value for employees. For example, tailor topics to the interests and needs of the audience. If your company's history is part of your orientation, allow more time for focusing on the local level than the corporate level, because it is more relevant to your audience.

Is the company including a general orientation in its onboarding program?

Find out what topics are included in the orientation. (We include a list of suggested topics in chapter 4 under "Program Content for General Onboarding.") Learn about how much time the company dedicates to the general orientation component—a three-day orientation will likely yield different results than a one-day program. The amount of information presented during an orientation can be overwhelming for attendees, so you might want to consider dividing it into shorter units.

Does the company offer a general onboarding program for all positions?

If the answer is yes, the company is not considering the differences between roles that should be addressed in onboarding. This signifies an important starting point for building a case for a program that is differentiated by position and by role.

Does the company offer a differentiated program by position?

If the company differentiates the program by position, find out for which positions and how the company decides who participates, what is included in the differentiated program, and why this is so. A company may offer general onboarding, but has hourly employees attend sessions where individual contributors, supervisors, managers, and executives do not participate. Another company might offer role-specific onboarding for each position with or without a general onboarding component for all groups simultaneously or separately.

What is the content of the onboarding program?

Program content varies depending on multiple business circumstances. Therefore, ask follow-up questions to find out as much as you can about what is included and why. For example, one company may dedicate a day to present topics related to the business, another one spends an entire day discussing issues related to the employee handbook, and a third uses role play to practice customer service scenarios regardless of employee role because service is a business imperative.

For instance, banks spend considerable time illustrating situations that tellers may encounter in their interactions with customers. Hotels emphasize the history of how the brand started and evolved into the present, as well as detailing the importance of customer service and tours of the facilities. Hospitals highlight legal and compliance aspects such as the Health Insurance Portability and Accountability Act (HIPAA) and confidentiality.

Ask follow-up questions to find out as much as you can about what is included in your company's onboarding program and why.

PRO TIP

Include short videos of no more than three minutes, use images, emphasize points with color, tell stories, and include music in your onboarding programs. It can also help to provide materials to touch, use objects as much as possible, and introduce role-play situations for pairs to practice behaviors.

Who facilitates the onboarding program?

What are their roles in the process? Effective onboarding programs encompass the orchestrated involvement of multiple players and stakeholders. The selection of program facilitators will certainly make an indelible first impression on participants, who are more likely to believe the company values its employees if they see top-level managers participating in the program.

How is the company handling the needs of specific employee groups?

Whether the company has the same program for all employees or separates them out by groups, at some point it will have to address the needs of specific employee groups. For example, the complexity of information that needs to be conveyed to hourly manufacturing employees about company safety practices is decidedly different from the level of detail required by hourly employees in administrative roles.

When does the onboarding program start and end?

Some companies define beginning and ending times for their onboarding programs based on the duration of the general group sessions if that is all that they offer. In contrast, other companies may include the duration of role-specific onboarding components, which depend on the complexity of the role. As a general rule, for most positions an onboarding program lasts between three months and one year.

For example, the onboarding program for a fast food worker may last two weeks, compared with one for a legal administrative assistant, which may last one month; someone in a supervisory or individual contributor role could spend six months in onboarding, and a vice president or executive could spend a year in onboarding.

Always pursue as much specificity as possible in terms of program duration and as it pertains to the different program components.

When are employees expected to be ready to perform their jobs?

Employee readiness varies depending on employee characteristics, background, and job specifics. Onboarding programs are a starting point for job readiness; employees who complete onboarding programs are usually ready to perform in less time than those who do not.

PRO TIP

Before you select your program's facilitators, ensure that they can transfer knowledge and are very articulate by observing them delivering training sessions and presentations. Once they're selected, take them through train-the-trainer sessions for practice, and conduct rehearsals for further observation and coaching.

How does the expectation of employee readiness to perform their jobs compare with their actual performance?

What is the relationship between company expectations about employee readiness to do their jobs and actual results? In our experience, employees are usually performing within one year of onboarding. If employees are meeting performance expectations, onboarding is likely a success factor, although it cannot be the only one. However, the program demands careful analysis if those employees are not meeting the company's readiness expectations and delivering results after participating in the role-specific component.

How does the company evaluate the results of the onboarding program?

Program evaluation is the key to finding out the impact of a business initiative. Its results are also useful to make a case for maintaining, expanding, or eliminating programs (or specific components), especially when comparing outcomes against initial investments. Further, companies that evaluate their programs are communicating the value they place on those programs. If the company is not evaluating its results, it is wasting an opportunity to obtain valuable data about its investment and information that can be used to improve the program. If the company does evaluate those results, request them because they should reveal information about what needs to change and what needs to stay the same when you revise the program.

Does the company track the engagement levels of employees who participated in the onboarding program?

Higher employee engagement levels are among the benefits of onboarding programs.

Measuring and monitoring the engagement levels of program participants is one way to monitor program effectiveness, especially when compared with the engagement levels of employees who did not participate in such programs. This serves a twofold purpose: to adjust the current program and to make a business case to revise it. Sort the engagement data by tenure in the company; those employees who report tenure of one year or less will be your recently onboarded employees.

PRO TIP

Consider including questions about onboarding in your next engagement survey, such as:

» Based on your onboarding experience, what can be improved to help new employees engage more quickly?

» Based on your onboarding experience or what you have heard about our onboarding program, what do you think the likelihood is that the new hires will leave the company before their first anniversary?

» What three things would you include in the onboarding program to make new colleagues feel more welcome in your department?

What is the feedback of former onboarding participants?

This question seeks information from former program participants at Kirkpatrick's Level 1, Reaction, which could be obtained directly from them as well as from L&D or HR. Onboarded employees should be a primary source for feedback about the program during and after their participation. They can describe what they liked and did not like, what was useful and not useful, and, most important, how the program can be improved to make it more effective for future participants.

What has been the feedback of the program's facilitators? Is there a trend?

Because program facilitators are in direct contact with new or new-to-role employees, often over extended periods, they are a primary source of information for what happens during program components in qualitative and quantitative terms. Some

PRO TIP

Compare the feedback you receive from former onboarding participants with the company's turnover rates. Find out if employees are leaving the company because they are not satisfied with their onboarding experience.

may even be asked to evaluate participant job performance after different learning experiences, such as on-the-job training. As experts in their fields, program facilitators can add value when you're starting to update content and redefine tactics.

What experience do the managers who are involved in employee recruitment and selection have in developing others?

Managers are often involved in pre-onboarding and lead role-specific onboarding programs. Therefore, they must have experience and a willingness to develop others. Companies need to reconsider the participation of managers who lack experience developing others, are not willing to develop others, or lack the competencies or time to do so. You should either provide mechanisms for these managers to gain the required experience and competencies, such as training and coaching, or find better-qualified substitutes for them during the role-specific component of onboarding.

RESOURCE

"Time to Take Our Own Advice: Q&A With Elaine Biech," an interview by Ryann Ellis (2018), emphasizes the importance of knowing what we do and why we do it.

What business results can be attributed to the onboarding program?

Granting that business results cannot be attributed solely to onboarding programs, it is still possible to establish associations between program participation and business results. For example, the time to productivity of onboarded employees should be shorter than that of employees who were not onboarded. The number and frequency of errors in tasks assigned should be lower among employees who were onboarded than among those who were not. The customer service indices of employees who were onboarded should be higher than those who were not. The dollar amount of new accounts brought in by onboarded employees should be greater than that of those employees who were not.

What are the program's strengths, weaknesses, opportunities, and threats?

The classic SWOT analysis serves to bring together different factors that have and may have an impact on the company's onboarding program. This is a question that lends itself to discussion in individual or group settings, and is useful to examine internal and external factors that can be at best modified and at worst anticipated as you revise your company's program. You may even be able to anticipate potential roadblocks for program implementation success based on the results of this analysis.

TOOL

The "Sample and Template for SWOT Analysis" at the end of this chapter, gives you a structure to organize the information you gather from your program's SWOT analysis.

What is the current political, economic, social, and technological environment surrounding the program?

How are those factors affecting it? This question addresses a different angle of the program's context than the previous question suggested, and lends itself to be asked in individual or group settings using the traditional PEST analysis. The answers typically elicit details about the broader context in which the organization operates, and which affect the current and desired state of the onboarding program. For example, any expected changes in technology within the company's industry will demand different competencies among new employees and diverse tactics to prepare these employees for their roles. In addition, any shifts in the demographic profiles of the available talent pool may lead to modifications in training approaches.

TOOL

The "Sample and Template for PEST Analysis," located at the end of this chapter, simplifies organizing the information you gather from your program's PEST analysis.

Path 2: The Company Does Not Have an Onboarding Program in Place

Did the company have an onboarding program in the past? If so, what type of program was it?

If the company had an onboarding program at some point, collect as many specific examples as possible of what it did.

Why did the company discontinue the onboarding program?

The answers to this question will allow you to identify some potential opportunities and roadblocks for the new program. For instance, the previous program may have been discontinued because the organization did not see its value, which points to an issue of evaluation that you will need to consider. The program could have been discontinued because no one was available to facilitate it and follow through. Or perhaps the company did not have the time to do it, which may suggest lack of support from management. In this case, you will need to focus on defining the desired state.

TOOL

The "Interview Guide to Define the Current State if the Company Does Not Have an Onboarding Program," located at the end of this chapter, can serve as a starting point to gather information.

How ready is the organization for an employee onboarding program?
By asking this question, you will define the program's scope and scale based on its current capabilities from the beginning, because organizations are rarely ready to launch full-blown onboarding programs. Consider designing and implementing your onboarding program by stages, and positioning each subsequent stage on the successes of the previous one.

Phase 2: Defining the Onboarding Program's Desired State

The information you gathered during Phase 1 gives you a solid foundation of where the organization stands regarding the onboarding program's current state. Now you are ready to define the program's desired state. The following set of questions will prompt you to think about what the company expects of its future onboarding program.

What is the company's vision for the future of the onboarding program?
Starting with a general picture of what the company expects of the onboarding program will guide you as you explore the specifics of those expectations in subsequent questions.

TOOL

The "Interview Guide to Define the Onboarding Program's Desired State," located at the end of the chapter, targets critical issues to define the program's desired state.

This general picture of the desired state will be critical when you complete the gap analysis in phase 3. The answers to this question will also give you a glimpse of how close or distant the current and desired states are, especially when getting into finer points, such as time and resources.

What specific company needs should the program address?

As program designer, you need to understand the business needs underlying the company's intention to have an onboarding program. In chapter 2 we introduced several benefits of an onboarding program. Clarify if the company already has some of those benefits in mind, if it is expecting something specific, or if an onboarding program is even the most appropriate way to meet those needs. Answers such as wanting "employees who can deliver results faster" or "employees who are committed to working here" are needs aligned with the purpose of an onboarding program; answers such as wanting to "have employees who are creative" signal misunderstanding of what an onboarding program can do, because creativity is a trait that onboarding cannot give the employee.

What does the company want to achieve with this program?

This question is closely related to the ones about the vision for the program and the needs that the company wants to address. Examine what the company wants to achieve with this program in the future, and translate that into a goal, which you'll express following the SMART format discussed in phase 1.

RESOURCE

Erika Lamont and Anne Bruce's *The Talent Selection and Onboarding Pocket Toolkit* (2004) is a good overview of the changing talent selection and onboarding landscape, and how to develop employees.

What business metrics does the company want to affect through this program?

For example, a company may be interested in reducing absenteeism among new employees. Another company may be interested in increasing productivity among new employees. Onboarding programs are a suitable means to have an impact on both metrics.

What business changes in the near future is the company anticipating that would have an impact on the goal and design of the onboarding program?

This question is closely related to those that addressed the organization's strengths, weaknesses, opportunities, and threats, as well as the political, environmental, social, and technological environment you identified for the current state using the SWOT and PEST analyses. Define "future" in number of years, as businesses commonly do. Consider completing SWOT and PEST analyses for a three-year timeframe. For example, the company may be expecting to increase or decrease the size of its workforce because of an acquisition, divestiture, new product introduction, or legacy product transfer. Because any of these changes would redefine the size and scope of the new workforce, they would also lead to rethinking the scope and goal of the program.

Who is the intended audience of the new program?

This question is designed to find out if the company is considering an onboarding program for a particular group or for all new hires, as well as a role-specific component for new-to-role employees or only for new external hires. Ask about the characteristics of these potential groups to get more specificity on the intended audience for the program.

Who will own the employee onboarding program?

Regardless of if the company expects the program's owner to change or stay the same, ask follow-up questions that will help you find reasons for either case. These will also shed light into program components that may or may not be working as expected. For example, inquire about what should stay the same and what should be different in the desired state, regardless of who owns the program.

How many employees does the company expect to hire in a given period?

A smaller number of anticipated new employees may call for a more individualized approach, even for the general onboarding phase; a larger number, on the other hand, may allow for a combination of large and small group components. Moreover, the number of expected hires, added to the number of anticipated employees whose roles will change, will represent onboarding program complexity. Regardless of anticipated group size, consistency in program delivery is what will make a difference in your program's success.

For what departments and positions is the company expecting to hire?

The areas and roles for which the company is expecting to bring new or new-to-role employees will become the priorities for the onboarding program. For example, a company that is expecting to increase the size of a call center may hire large numbers of customer service representatives whose profiles are very similar, while one that is developing new business lines will bring in employees with different backgrounds to perform different functions. The desired state for the first company's general onboarding program will entail one program for all new customer service representatives and a role-specific program that will be very similar for all participants. In contrast, the desired state of the second company's onboarding program will probably involve a general onboarding component that will be delivered to groups of only hourly employees and another to groups of individual contributors, supervisors, and managers. In addition, the desired state for the role-specific component of the second company's program will demand careful differentiation in design and duration by function and level. Therefore, the functions these employees would be expected to perform will determine which role-specific experiences and resources will be needed.

What is the anticipated demographic profile of new employees?

The multiple generations co-existing in the workforce is a relevant issue to define in your onboarding program's desired state. Knowing the demographic profile is important because the company will need to customize according to background and experience within the program's general and role-specific components.

Where will those employees be located?

Onboarding programs have to be designed within the context of the company's location, whether this means a site or a geographical area. The company has to further consider external cultural issues related to the location or nuances related to functions within a site or site's surrounding area, such as small town versus metropolitan, to facilitate the transitions of those employees. For example, employees who work for a company based in the United States have a different work experience than those who work for a company in Central America or Europe, even if it is the same U.S.-based company.

What type of employment experience are new hires or new-to-role employees looking for?

As today's workforce continues to change and so much information about companies and roles within them is available online, employees develop expectations about their employment experience that go beyond job security and basic benefits. Many of today's employees are seeking opportunities to grow professionally, understanding that this growth may come from nontraditional career paths, and personally by becoming involved in social responsibility initiatives.

Many employees are looking for an environment where they can establish close connections with others and belong to a community. In contrast, other employees are looking for flexibility and autonomy to complete their work without schedule or location restrictions. Still others prefer traditional and structured environments where roles and responsibilities are clearly established and chains of command must be followed. Knowing the type of employment experience that newcomers seek is important from the beginning of the recruitment and selection process as the company decides if the candidate is a good fit for the company. This information also prompts onboarding program design decisions because the program has to reflect the company culture and brand.

Who are the program stakeholders?

Identifying who these stakeholders will be as well as pinpointing those who will be involved in employee onboarding for the first time will serve to map how they will be prepared for their participation within the parameters of the new program. Pay special attention to any expected changes in stakeholder groups or individuals involved.

Will the new program include an orientation component?

What will that involve? The content of the orientation component and the level of detail expected to be included will shed light on the company's commitment to the program. Be on the lookout for dismissals (for example, "we don't need an orientation") as well as for extremes in expectations for content (either too little or too much), because you will need to influence program managers to grasp the importance of including an orientation component with the right amount of content for its intended audience.

Who will facilitate the program and how will each facilitator contribute?

As a general rule, L&D facilitates onboarding unless the business requires otherwise. Besides the specific data that you obtain about facilitators and their contributions for the program's desired state, through this question you will be able to indirectly gauge the company's current satisfaction with its slate of facilitators. Any anticipated changes in facilitators from the current to the desired state will suggest that you will need to determine if they have the necessary competencies for the role and that you prepare new ones for participation in the program.

Phase 3: Analyzing the Gap

You are now ready to organize what you learned about the company's current program (the current state), if one exists, and compare it with what you learned about what the company expects for the new program (the desired state). The results of the comparisons you make will become your gap analysis. They are the foundation of what you need to do to get your company's onboarding program to its desired state, which you will define in phase 4 at a high level. You will develop that design further after your company approves your business case. Summarize the information that you gathered as you were asking questions about the program's current and desired states so the story behind your data emerges.

TOOL

The "Sample and Template to Compare the Onboarding Program's Current and Desired States," located at the end of the chapter, can be used to summarize the current and desired states and then identify the gap between them.

As you summarize, consider what you learned about components of the current and desired programs. Look for similarities and differences between the elements of the current and desired states of the program that you listed, such as metrics. How close or far apart these elements are will affect the scope of the program in terms of the amount and type of work that will need to be done to close the gap. For instance, if the current state's vision is very similar to the desired state's vision, refocusing or redesigning some components may be sufficient, unless the company is overlooking some fundamental components that must be included. If so, you will need to bring up those components in the business case for the new program. If these elements are totally different, closing this gap will demand a program overhaul or a completely new program, and the interests of the organization may be best served by developing and launching such a program in stages.

Phase 4: Closing the Gap

Use the results of the gap analysis to determine the new program's goal and the type of program you are going to design. The new onboarding program could take one of many forms, either from its outset or after a series of stages. Each form has advantages and disadvantages that must be considered to decide which option would the best for your company.

TOOL

Use the "Templates for Analysis of the Advantages and Disadvantages of Programs" tool at the end of this chapter to summarize the results of your analysis of each type of program as they pertain to your business. This will help you determine which approach would be best.

When deciding what program component or combination of components to include in your program, consider the following advantages and disadvantages of each. Let's look at the different combinations.

Some advantages of pre-onboarding for new and new-to-role employees include getting documents and paperwork completed and preparing the organization to receive those employees. They can also be introduced to other employees during pre-onboarding events, which means they'll recognize familiar faces when onboarding starts and when they arrive at their specific areas. However, if the starting dates change, if they withdraw from the process, or if they reject the employment or position offer at the last minute, these efforts will have been wasted.

Including a general orientation as part of general onboarding for new employees provides common content for all, allows them to obtain a general understanding of the business, and addresses cultural issues in broad terms because these orientations are usually focused on the company. However, general content tends to be wide-ranging and superficial for reaching audiences with a variety of backgrounds and roles. It may also center on rules and compliance issues that may not be relevant to everyone. Moreover, because of the content's nature, these orientations often cannot account for intradepartment cultural or role-specific differences. Participants may also feel isolated from the rest of the company if they only interact with other new employees.

Delivering general onboarding for new-to-role employees provides up-to-date information about the industry and the business. This may result in a shortened time to productivity because they already have a basic understanding of the company's culture. However, the nature of this component asks for specificity that can only be achieved through pointed individual development.

General onboarding for new hourly employees and customized onboarding for others with specific roles, such as supervisors, managers, and executives, requires some degree of customization by offering business and industry information, as well as general company and specific department cultural information that is tailored to employee level, role, and profile. This customization allows supervisors, managers, and executives to access the resources that are valuable for their long-term development. Notwithstanding, this approach may maintain a separation between new and new-to-role employees, with the former perceiving inequities if they notice that new-to-role employees are not being onboarded.

General onboarding for hourly new-to-role employees, combined with customized role-specific onboarding for new-to-role supervisors, managers, and executives, addresses the role-specific needs of each group, including those topics related to unique cultural issues. However, although this approach caters to the individual needs of supervisors, managers, and executives, it still eclipses those of hourly employees, who may claim that their role transitions are more complex.

General onboarding for new and new-to-role employees with a general orientation and role-specific components, regardless of levels, provides common content for all participants and anchors everyone's understanding of the business's culture. This gives participants a foundation for grasping the nuances of department subcultures during role-specific onboarding. This approach acknowledges the importance of all roles for business success while granting access to individual development resources according to role and organizational level. It also serves to recognize and account for individual differences. Nevertheless, because of its direct relation with the business, this take on onboarding demands constant review and updating, as well as the availability of a wide range of resources, possibly including third parties, who must be prepared to deliver the role-specific components and whose transitions must be coordinated smoothly. When a company's financial and human resources allow it, general onboarding for new and new-to-role employees along with role-specific onboarding for all levels is the best option.

Phase 5: Building Your Business Case

The business case serves to tell the company what you plan to do and how much the company will need to invest to make it a reality. It brings together the benefits, drawbacks, risks, costs, current situation, and future state. The purpose of the business case is to get approval; by doing so, you make onboarding a business priority.

It is a communications tool and, as such, L&D has to frame it using the language of the company.

Typically, the business case answers the following questions:

- Why is onboarding important for the company?
- Where is the company in terms of onboarding?
- Why does the company need an onboarding program?
- What are some potential benefits of an onboarding program for the company?
- What does the company want to achieve with an onboarding program?
- What are the essential components of an onboarding program?
- How and when will stakeholders participate?
- How much will the program cost?
- How long will the program take to implement?

To prepare the business case, start with a summary of your organizational assessment (that is, what you did, how you collected information, and the highlights of the results). Then establish a relationship between the current and desired state based on those results, which will lead to delineating the program's scope in terms of:

- audience (new employees, new-to-role employees, executives, employee demographics, employee skill level, employee schedules)
- phases (pre-onboarding, general onboarding, role-specific onboarding)
- orientation content
- facilitators
- delivery methods (face-to-face, online, blended).

Next, you will introduce the connection between the program and the company's key performance indicators related to people (Figure 3-3). For example, under Reduce Turnover Rate, you want to verify and communicate the company's turnover rate before and after the inception of your program.

PRO TIP

Always include powerful statistics. They speak the language of business.

Figure 3-3. Topics to Show Value of Onboarding Program

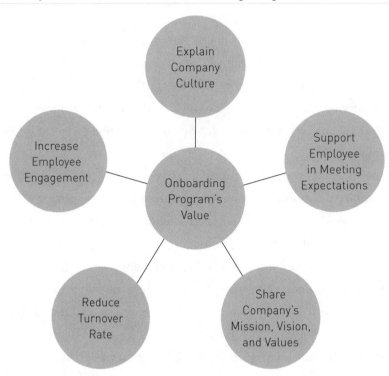

Next, you will justify why the program is important and why it needs to be implemented. Last, you will provide estimated costs of design and implementation.

A business case usually contains the following sections: executive summary, context, purpose, benefits, objectives and goals, project description, estimated timeline, financial investment, and next steps. Let's take a closer look at each.

TOOL

The "Template for Business Case," located at the end of this chapter, will help you organize the information that you collected to build your business case.

Executive Summary

The executive summary is a short version of the business case, which allows readers to rapidly become acquainted with a large amount of content. Your executive summary needs to drive the reader to read the rest of the document. It answers the question of why the company should onboard its employees.

Context

The context portion presents the current business situation, as well as the company's or the program's strengths and gaps in onboarding.

Purpose

This section answers the question of why company needs onboarding. It should include statistics, such as the costs of losing an employee before the first year of employment, turnover over a set period, comparisons of employee retention in companies that do and don't have onboarding programs, and average tenure of onboarded versus non-onboarded employees. (See chapter 5 for other metrics.)

Benefits

The benefits section is where you highlight the value an onboarding program adds to the company. Chapter 2 outlined some of the benefits of onboarding programs that could be relevant for your business case. For instance, the company may reduce costs by aligning the onboarding program to the business strategy and reducing turnover rates.

Objectives and Goals

This section introduces what the company intends to achieve through an onboarding program in measurable terms.

Project Description

This is the longest section of the business case. It should include the program's goals and objectives in SMART terms, as well as who will be involved in the program and their roles, the activities that will be delivered, and the preliminary measures of success the company will use.

PRO TIP

When you map the picture of your program in the business case, be sure to include all information needed to get its approval. Anticipate your audience's possible questions based on their interests and needs.

Estimated Timeline

This section presents a proposed sequence of activities with a suggested timeframe, a general implementation schedule, immediate and long-term steps with approximate milestones, and who will be doing what and when.

Financial Investment

The financial investment section is directed at those who will approve the project's budget. It provides information about the financial implications of the onboarding program, allowing the company to compare associated costs and anticipated benefits. Make sure that the project is financially feasible within the company's situation.

Next Steps

To close your business case, include a description of what the company will do to start the onboarding program.

PRO TIP

Anticipate all possible reactions when putting together your business case. You can do this by following company guidelines and practices, minimizing the use of jargon, and preparing to handle objections.

Now You Have the Foundation

Having your business case approved makes onboarding a priority. It shows that your onboarding program is a critical business initiative to generate business improvement that results in real value. You now have the foundation to design your onboarding program. In the next chapter we will discuss how to develop and implement the onboarding program for your organization.

Questions to Explore:

- Does your company have an onboarding program? Why or why not?
- With whom do you need to meet to gather the information required to complete your organizational assessment?

- How can you influence stakeholders to participate in the organizational assessment?
- How would you describe the current state of your company's onboarding program?
- Who participates in the company's onboarding program? Why?
- Who is the audience for the company's onboarding program?
- What specific need does the company intend to address with this program?
- What will you do to convince the company to do role-specific onboarding?
- Whom do you need to convince first to revise (or design) an onboarding program for the company?
- How would you describe the desired state of your company's onboarding program?
- What combination of components will you use for your company's onboarding program?
- What is the main challenge you will face to take the company's program from its current to its desired state?
- What will you do to address that challenge?
- What will you include in your business case?
- What issues or concerns may top management have about your business case for onboarding? What can you do to address them?

Tools for Support

Interview Guide to Define Current State if Company Has Onboarding Program

Does your company already have an onboarding program in place? If so, you'll follow path 1. Use these questions to help define the current state of the program.

- When was the last time that the company's onboarding program or new employee orientation program was revised and updated and why?
- What is the company's vision for the onboarding program?
- What does the company want to achieve with this program?
- What does the company do to welcome and ease the transition of new employees into the organization?
- Who is the owner of the employee onboarding program?
- Who are the stakeholders of the program?
- How are recruitment and selection involved in the onboarding program?
- Is the onboarding program designed only for new employees who are external hires, or does it also include those current employees or transfers who are assuming new roles?
- Is the company including a general orientation in its onboarding program?
- Does the company offer a general onboarding program for all positions?
- Does the company offer a differentiated program by position?
- What is the content of the onboarding program?
- Who facilitates the onboarding program? What are their roles in the process?
- How is the company handling the needs of specific employee groups?
- When does the onboarding program start and end?
- When are employees expected to be ready to perform their jobs?
- How does the expectation of employee readiness to perform their jobs compare with their actual performance?
- How does the company evaluate the results of the onboarding program?

- Does the company track the engagement levels of employees who participated in the onboarding program?
- What is the feedback of former participants of the onboarding program?
- What is the feedback of the program's facilitators? Is there a trend?
- What experience do the managers who are involved in employee recruitment and selection have in developing others?
- What business results can be attributed to the onboarding program?
- What are the program's strengths, weaknesses, opportunities, and threats?
- What is the political, economic, social, and technological environment that surrounds the program? How are those factors affecting the program?

Sample and Template for SWOT Analysis

The SWOT analysis brings together the strengths, weaknesses, opportunities, and threats that are having and may have an impact on the company's onboarding program. Use the sample to see how it works, and then use the template to organize the information you gather from your program's SWOT analysis.

Sample SWOT Analysis

	Positive	Negative
Internal	**Strengths** Effective partnership between L&D and HR (facilitates design and delivery of program based on complementarity)	**Weaknesses** Pool of facilitators is very limited and are dedicated to regulatory training (need to select and prepare additional facilitators)
External	**Opportunities** Increase in number of graduates from a nearby university with degrees relevant to meet business needs (creates larger pool of available candidates for entry-level positions and onboarding has to consider their profile in program design)	**Threats** New government regulations (affect content and duration of role-specific onboarding)

SWOT Analysis Template

	Positive	Negative
Internal	Strengths	Weaknesses
External	Opportunities	Threats

Sample and Template for PEST Analysis

Use the PEST analysis to determine the political, economic, social, and technological factors that could have an impact on your onboarding program. Use the example analysis to see how it works and then use the template to organize the information you gather from your own PEST analysis.

Sample PEST Analysis

Political	Economic
• Approval of law increasing minimum wage (affects employee profile and increases hiring costs) • Increase in government regulations for industry segment (affects content of role-specific onboarding)	• Decreased unemployment rate in region (may be more difficult and costly to find the right employees for the company)
Social	**Technological**
• Multiple generations co-existing in the workplace (onboarding has to address all generations' learning preferences)	• Company moving to online delivery of training programs (affects design of the onboarding program)

PEST Analysis Template

Political	Economic
Social	**Technological**

Interview Guide to Define the Current State if the Company Does Not Have an Onboarding Program

Does your company already have an onboarding program in place? If not, you'll follow path 2. Use these questions as a starting point to gather information to define what, if anything, the company is doing to ease the transition of employees into the workplace.

- Did the company have an onboarding program in the past? If so, what type of program was it? Who owned and facilitated the program?
- Why did the company discontinue the onboarding program?
- How ready is the organization for an employee onboarding program?

Interview Guide to Define the Onboarding Program's Desired State

Once you have a solid foundation of where the organization stands regarding the current state of the onboarding program, you need to define the program's desired state. Use these questions to help you define what the company expects of the future onboarding program.

- What is the company's vision of the onboarding program's future?
- What specific company needs should the program address?
- What will the company want to achieve with this program?
- On what business metrics does the company want to have an impact through this program?
- What business changes in the near future is the company anticipating that would have an impact on the goal and design of the onboarding program?
- Who is the intended audience of the new program?
- Who will own the employee onboarding program?
- How many employees does the company expect to hire in a given period?
- For what departments and positions is the company expecting to hire?
- What is the anticipated demographic profile of those employees?
- Where would those employees be located?
- What type of employment experience are new hires or new-to-role employees looking for?
- Will the new program include an orientation component? What are the orientation components?
- Who will facilitate the onboarding program and how will each facilitator contribute?

Sample and Template to Compare the Onboarding Program's Current and Desired States

Use this chart to summarize the current and desired states and then identify the gap between the two. Use the sample comparison as an example as you fill in the template provided here.

Sample Comparison

Current State	Desired State	Difference or Gap
Owner: HR	Owner: L&D	New expected owner
Orientation for all new employees	Orientation for new and new-to-role employees differentiated by groups	Orientation will include more groups and will be different
Not tracking employee engagement	Will track employee engagement	New measure
Participants do not report understanding role after program completion	Participants expected to understand and perform role after program completion	Expectation of job performance for onboarded employees

Template for Your Comparison

Current State	Desired State	Difference or Gap

Templates for Analysis of the Advantages and Disadvantages of Programs

Look at the advantages and disadvantages of each program component or combination for your company to decide which one will be more viable now. Consider paving the way to more encompassing approaches as the needs and readiness of your company evolve.

Pre-Onboarding Programs for New Employees and New-to-Role Employees

Program Component/ Combination	Advantages	Disadvantages	What to Include
Pre-onboarding for new employees			
Pre-onboarding for new-to-role employees			

General Onboarding Programs for New Employees and New-to-Role Employees

Program Component/ Combination	Advantages	Disadvantages	What to Include
General onboarding for new employees with general orientation			
General onboarding for new-to-role employees			

General Onboarding Programs for Hourly New Employees and Customized Onboarding for Employees With Specific Roles

Program Component/ Combination	Advantages	Disadvantages	What to Include
General onboarding for hourly new employees, combined with customized onboarding for new employees with specific roles such as supervisors, managers, and executives			
General onboarding for hourly new-to-role employees combined with customized onboarding for new-to-role employees, such as supervisors, managers, and executives			

General Onboarding Programs for New Employees and New-to-Role Employees with Role-Specific Onboarding Regardless of Level

Program Component/ Combination	Advantages	Disadvantages	What to Include
General onboarding for everyone, including a general orientation, combined with role-specific onboarding for everyone regardless of level			

Template for Business Case

A business case usually contains an executive summary, context, purpose, benefits, objectives and goals, a project description, an estimated timeline, the financial investment, and next steps. Use this tool to help organize the information that you collect as you build your business case.

Executive Summary
Context
Purpose
Benefits
Objectives and Goals
Project Description
Estimated Timeline
Financial Investment
Next Steps

Additional Resources

Achor, S. 2011. "The Happy Secret to Better Work." TEDx Talk, May. www.ted.com /talks/shawn_achor_the_happy_secret_to_better_work/transcript?language=en.

Barghelame, K. 2016. "What Maslow's Hierarchy of Needs Can Teach Us About Employee Onboarding." Gusto, June 29. https://gusto.com/framework/hr /what-maslows-hierarchy-of-needs-can-teach-us-employee-onboarding.

Buttrick, R. 2009. *The Project Workout: The Ultimate Handbook of Project and Program Management*, 4th ed. New York: Prentice Hall.

Ellis, R. 2018. "Time to Take Our Own Advice: Q&A With Elaine Biech." ATD Insights, February 28. www.td.org/insights/time-to-take-our-own-advice-q-a -with-elaine-biech.

Friedman, J.P., ed. 2007. *Dictionary of Business Terms*, 4th ed. Hauppaugue, NY: Barron's Educational Services.

Gide, A. 2018. "André Gide." Wikipedia, June 14. https://en.wikipedia.org/wiki /Andr%C3%A9_Gide.

Hogan, M. 2015. "How to Get Employee Onboarding Right." *Forbes*, May 29. www .forbes.com/sites/theyec/2015/05/29/how-to-get-employee-onboarding-right /#2cae3fb0407b.

HR|Onboard. 2017. *The Five Pillars of a Great Onboarding Program.* HR|Onboard. https:// hronboard.me/wp-content/uploads/2017/06/Five-pillars-of-onboarding.pdf.

Lamont, E., and A. Bruce. 2014. *The Talent Selection and Onboarding Pocket Toolkit.* New York: McGraw-Hill Education.

Maurer, R. 2017. "New Employee Onboarding Guide." Society for Human Resource Management. www.shrm.org/resourcesandtools/hr-topics/talent-acquisition /pages/new-employee-onboarding-guide.aspx.

Pastakia, K., and S. Harrington. n.d. "The Future of Work—A Reorientation Guide." Deloitte. www2.deloitte.com/content/dam/Deloitte/ca/Documents/human -capital/ca-en-future-of-work.pdf.

Patel, S. 2015. "How to Create an Effective Onboarding Experience at Your Startup." *Forbes,* March 11. www.forbes.com/sites/sujanpatel/2015/03/11/how-to-create-an -effective-onboarding-experience-at-your-startup.

Pignatelli, A. 2016. "What Maslow Would Say About Employee Motivation Today?" HR.com, May 8. www.hr.com/en/magazines/recognition_engagement_excellence _essentials/may_2016_recognition_engagement/what-maslow-would-say-about -employee-motivation-to_inypdzjk.html.

Saavides, S., and S. Rogers. 2017. "Onboarding as a Priority on Your Talent Agenda: Why You Need a Future-Proof Approach to the New Hire Journey." Deloitte. www2.deloitte.com/nl/nl/pages/human-capital/articles/onboarding-as-a-priority -on-your-talent-agenda.html.

Shim, J.K., and J.G. Siegel. 2010. *Dictionary of Accounting Terms,* 5th ed. Hauppaugue, NY: Barron's Educational Services.

SHRM (Society for Human Resource Management). 2017. "Managing the Employee Onboarding and Assimilation Process." SHRM, March 6. www.shrm.org/resources andtools/tools-and-samples/toolkits/pages/onboardingandassimilationprocess.aspx.

Sullivan, J. 2015. "Extreme Onboarding: How to WOW Your New Hires Rather Than Numb Them." LinkedIn Talent Blog, July 15. https://business.linkedin.com/talent -solutions/blog/2015/07/extreme-onboarding-how-to-wow-your-new-hires-rather -than-numb-them.

You presented the business case for the program and received approval to develop and implement what you proposed. You now are ready to implement your company's onboarding program, equipped with the results of the organizational assessment, the company's goal for the program, and the general choices that the company made about which program to pursue.

As a key element of successful talent management strategies, onboarding must be carefully planned, reviewed, and tailored to meet the needs and background of your audience as well as the current business strategies and business environment every time it is offered. Pre-onboarding, general onboarding, and role-specific onboarding will need to be integrated into a seamless continuum.

Onboarding, as a company-wide effort, cannot be accomplished without support from other departments and business units. Groups such as facilities, information systems, security, payroll, and finance will need to be involved behind the scenes to make the program successful. Secure their support and involvement to ensure that they will deliver the services that you need. Involve representatives from those groups in discussions about the program to receive their feedback and

TOOL

The "Department Support Checklist," located at the end of this chapter, will help you track the status of what you need from other company departments for onboarding.

enhance their ownership of the process. Use a checklist to keep track of what you need from those departments to ensure the flawless delivery of your program.

General Preparations for Onboarding

Depending on the number of expected hires, their positions, and the extent of the program's scope, you will need to consider the elements shown in Table 4-1. Make sure that you script what happens in each component with clear roles and responsibilities.

TOOL

The "Onboarding Checklist," located at the end of this chapter, takes managers step by step through the entire onboarding process, detailing what they need to do and the topics that they need to discuss.

In these days of technological advances, global connectivity, and job transformations, it is not unusual to have someone working in Singapore and reporting to someone located in London. Some employees perform highly specialized functions that do not require frequent face-to-face interactions. Others work this way because of the nature of the business, and can work from anywhere as long as they meet performance standards. Nonetheless, all new or new-to-role employees must be onboarded.

Table 4-1. Onboarding Program Design Elements

Design Element	Pre-Onboarding	General Onboarding	Role-Specific Onboarding
Program Content	X	X	X
Program Duration	X	X	X
Approximate Dates and Times	X	X	X
Logistics	X	X	X
Large vs. Small Settings	X	X	X
Individual Meetings	X		X
Communications	X	X	X
Content of Presentations and Exercises		X	
Delivery Methods		X	X
Facilitators		X	X
Training for Facilitators		X	X
Consistency in Branding	X	X	X
Top Management Participation		X	
Progress and Logistics Checkpoints	X	X	X
Support From Other Departments	X	X	X

Pre-Onboarding

Organizations recruit candidates for positions to meet their current and future business needs. They seek credentials and experience for success in the position; they also seek cultural fit through the interview process. HR manages the pre-onboarding phase and partners with the employee's manager to define the need for the position and find the best candidate for it. HR also handles all transactions related to employee benefits, company policies, security, and compliance issues such as leave, work schedule, and the employee handbook.

The employee's manager participates in the interviewing process and, because they will be working directly with the employee, the quality of that relationship will be a determining factor in the employee's performance and engagement. The manager's presence and availability during the onboarding process delivers a message of welcome and support to the employee.

Assuming that the candidate selected for the position, whether external or internal, met these criteria, the pre-onboarding phase begins when they accept the offer. This acceptance also marks the start of L&D's customization of the general onboarding phase and of the manager's planning for the role-specific phase, based on the profile of each new employee.

Companies can capitalize on the time between the offer acceptance and first day of the new or new-to-role employee by initiating and maintaining continuity in onboarding. Use this transition time to get to know the new or new-to-role employee as an individual to begin building trust while HR handles the administrative tasks, such as completing profiles, registering for benefits, and requesting information from the employee. Consider granting access to company websites and sharing invitations to targeted company events for those in managerial and executive positions.

PRO TIP

Have employees complete any new-hire paperwork, whether online or face-to-face, during pre-onboarding to get this task out of the way.

Through these initial interactions, HR and L&D can identify the employee's development needs and learning preferences as well as the most important drivers of the new or new-to-role employee's engagement if these did not emerge during the interview process. Some of these drivers for engagement are the manager-employee relationship, intrinsic motivation, leadership, performance management, career development, financial or external incentives, organizational image and brand, and brand alignment (Dávila and Piña-Ramírez 2013). Establishing priorities among those drivers will be useful when tailoring role-specific onboarding.

The moment when the candidate accepts the employment offer becomes a golden opportunity to provide company information through a well-crafted welcome packet highlighting the company brand and its meaning. Consider preparing versions of the packet, or some of its content, in other languages, audio versions, or larger fonts to address any special needs.

TOOL

At the end of this chapter, you'll find suggested contents for a new employee welcome packet. You'll also find a sample email that less formal workplace environments could use to communicate with the employee to be onboarded.

HR and L&D will continue to gather information valuable to preparing the employee profile for general onboarding and tailor the proportion of presentations and exercises or interactive activities to suit employee needs, as well as details for role-specific onboarding.

Every contact with the employee is an opportunity to introduce and reinforce company culture messages; therefore, everyone who will have contact with the employee has to be ready to serve as company ambassador 24/7. All employees, regardless of role, must be aware of the importance of onboarding. Share with them the latest information about the business.

HR communicates the arrival of the new or new-to-role employee to all other interested parties such as finance, payroll, facilities, security, information systems, and reception. By ensuring identification cards are issued, system access is granted, telephone services are activated, and tools and equipment are assigned (such as desk space, cell phones, and computers), HR contributes to that positive first impression.

Other logistics that need to be handled during pre-onboarding include confirming appointments, requesting documents, sending directions or dropping a pin to make sure that new or new-to-role employees know where to go, assigning special parking arrangements, setting up conference rooms, and creating welcome packets and other materials. These all send the message that the company cares about its new employees. Build in progress and logistics checkpoints to make sure that everything happens when it should.

PRO TIP

Send a welcome note to the employee's company email address the night before their first day so that they receive it as soon as they log in to the system.

General Onboarding

L&D leads general onboarding and partners with the employee's manager. It designs, facilitates, and monitors the onboarding components across organizational levels and functions. As experts in how people learn, L&D is the go-to resource of onboarding, able to tailor its components to meet individual needs. HR has to assume the responsibility of onboarding if the organization does not have an L&D function. If the organization does not have a formal HR function, managers or company owners have to be responsible for the onboarding process.

General onboarding is usually designed as a group experience for new or new-to-role employees who have not been onboarded in the last three to five years or are in supervisory, managerial, or executive roles. This allows them to come together to begin their assimilation into the company and its culture. A best practice is grouping employees who perform similar roles because they will likely have questions and concerns that are irrelevant to those in different roles. Top managers and executives undergo this type of experience through completely individualized programs.

Capitalize on the new employee's sense of wonder, pride, and excitement to create a strong bond between them and the company. This is another opportunity to build on your pre-onboarding successes.

Use every opportunity to reinforce the uniqueness of the company and what it offers. Leave a lasting positive memory on the onboarded employees to counteract any possibility of buyer's remorse after accepting the employment offer. The manager should be there to meet the new employee at the beginning of the day and then again at the end for a recap of the day's events; this conversation will likely be shared with those waiting at home, who will become their supporters during the entire onboarding process.

Let's meet Ian and see how this works in practice.

Ian's Story

Ian was eager to start work at a major telemarketer's call center. He was proud to have been selected from a group of 200 applicants for one of 20 positions. Because he was assigned to work during the first shift, he could even continue pursuing his undergraduate degree.

When Ian accepted the offer, his new manager told him that he would first attend a group orientation and then later receive individualized training to do his job.

Ian arrived on time for the group orientation, but then he had to wait for the receptionist to return to her station. She did not know about the meeting Ian was scheduled to attend, and did not know whom to contact to find out. Ian waited for more than 30 minutes before someone who could take him to his meeting arrived. Ian felt disregarded and lost.

The HR generalist who greeted Ian took him to a large empty room with 15 computers. She pointed him to a cubicle and gave him the code to access the Online Onboarding Portal to complete forms. He had been told he would attend a group session, so he was confused and wondered what was going on.

After spending three hours completing forms, Ian got up and went to get lunch by himself because no one was around. When he returned, he ran into the HR generalist, who said that he should have waited for her to go to lunch, even though no one had said anything to him about lunch plans.

The HR generalist then took Ian back to the computer room and told him to continue completing the forms. She said someone would come pick him up at 2:30 to attend a company meeting, but didn't offer any further explanation.

To minimize the possibility of a new employee having an experience like Ian's, you'll need to have answers to questions such as, who needs to know when a new employee arrives? Who should welcome the new employee to the organization? What information should the new employee receive before the first day?

Companies often establish hiring-date calendars to structure participation in group sessions before onboarded employees arrive at their departments or units. We recommend that employees participate in general onboarding no more than three days after they start, because supervisors and managers are often reluctant to allow attendance after new employees assume their responsibilities.

Program Content for General Onboarding

A general orientation has to create a "Wow!" experience that can impress a diverse audience; its content has to include elements that will make it meaningful across the board. As you establish the sequence of your orientation's content, be careful to avoid information overload. Divide and sequence the content in ways that participants can assimilate and own it. Consider structuring the agenda with group sessions in the mornings and training sessions in the afternoons over three to five days.

Even though regulatory and mandatory training requirements vary by industry and position, in general, companies train employees on:

- sexual harassment in the workplace
- diversity and inclusion
- safety and security
- emergency management and disaster recovery
- information management and confidentiality
- affirmative action
- handling domestic violence.

Decisions about approximate dates and times must consider critical business periods, such as month-end closing for finance departments and peak production periods for manufacturing operations. As you build consistency into your program, participants and stakeholders will be able to schedule their time and anticipate their involvement accordingly. We recommend having specific dates, such as the second Monday each month, when the company reaches a particular threshold of new or new-to-role employees.

Organizational history is often the starting point of new employee orientations. They are eager to hear how the business started and how it became what it is. They also want to know where the company is going, so the vision of the future must be part of the general orientation. New-to-role employees may have missed events or dismissed their significance at the time, so this gives them a second opportunity to appreciate them. Remember, everything is new for them because of the new role. This information, usually presented using a combination of media, heightens the employee's sense of belonging. Weave in how the company's values emerged, evolved, and are embodied as well as what made the company unique from its inception. Key policies, practices, and procedures can also be highlighted in this section and then discussed in greater detail at the department level during role-specific onboarding.

RESOURCE

For samples of compelling messages about companies, view the following videos:

» Coco—Inside Chanel (www.youtube.com/watch?v=2G88zqPxJ00)

» The History of Nike Brand Evolution (www.youtube.com/watch?v=MQNgJ2mpW9I).

It is important for a company's senior-level management and executives to partic-ipate in the program. They often welcome attendees and answer questions either in person or through telecommunications or videos. Their presence adds significance to the organizational history because many often have a prominent place in that history. Employees may look up to them and, by hearing their stories, envision a future for themselves in the organization. Living legends—such as a company founder who overcame significant obstacles or a successor who built on the legacy of the founder to take the business to new heights—make the organization's history real and available for all employees. Their consistent participation in onboarding programs sends a powerful message to the rest of the organization about the program's importance for the business.

RESOURCE

Melanie Padgett Powers (2016) shares lessons from government onboarding that you can adapt for your company in her article, "Power Switch: Onboarding Tips From the Experts Who Help New Presidents Fill 4,000-Plus Positions in Less Than 90 Days."

As much as possible, avoid having to cancel appointments or presentations at the last minute by scheduling them well in advance or finding appropriate substitutes during specific business periods. Try to prevent occurrences like Melody experienced in the following example.

Melody's Story

Melody was facilitating a session for a group of new employees who had recently joined the team at the mattress factory. They were all entry-level operators and, for many, this was their first work experience. They were eager to find out more about the company and hoping to meet its leaders.

After showing a slide with the pictures of all the top managers, Melody mentioned that one was going to come meet the group. However, in the middle of her presentation, she received a message saying that he would not be able to make it. What a way to make a first impression! What an awkward situation for Melody!

PRO TIP

Always have personal knowledge about the delivery capabilities of potential top management substitutes and make sure they meet your standards. Have video messages from key leaders available as backups if a good substitute isn't available.

Sometimes companies delegate the responsibility of representing top management at events such as general orientations. Whoever is delegated this responsibility has to be ready and confident to do so at a moment's notice. Otherwise, situations such as the following will require extra efforts to mitigate.

Henri's Story

Henri had always wanted to represent the company and speak in front of an audience. He had been preparing for a long time and had even taken acting classes to improve his demeanor onstage. His manager had already recognized Henri's potential as a successor and he had an individualized development plan to learn more about the business.

On the morning of the orientation when his manager was scheduled to speak, Henri received a phone call that he would need to step in and address the group. Henri accepted the challenge without giving it a second thought.

When introduced, Henri approached the front of the room. His hands were sweating and his voice cracked as he began to speak. He lost his train of thought twice and he had to cut the presentation short. The result? A major setback for Henri because he was not ready, and an even greater one for the company because the first impression the orientation's attendees received from top management was not a good one.

As a general onboarding practice, be prepared to highlight the company's locations, products and services, competitors, market share, major awards and recognitions, memorable and recent advertising campaigns, division contributions, and social responsibility, among other elements, that make the company unique. Bring samples of products for attendees to see or otherwise experience if your industry segment allows. For example, a manufacturer of baked goods can bring samples for employees to taste during coffee breaks. A bank can share promotional materials and videos about its products and services. A hospital can include patients' testimonials about their experience.

As employees learn the nature of the business, it is important for them to hear about financials. Introduce general information about company financials and metrics—trends that affect the business and its growth and are related to employees. Otherwise, you can include public information about revenues and the company's market share and market position.

Include a clear depiction of the company's strategic mission and reason for being, as well as its vision, where it wants to be, and how it will lead the way into the future, which will engender a sense of security among employees. These are central issues for the company because all its activities are driven toward fulfilling that mission and reaching that vision.

Company values are often the foundation of the company's culture. All employees need to understand and believe in them; the general orientation is the first of many instances when values can be brought to life as presenters model them and share examples of employees who embody them. Examples and stories, whether through live testimonials, video clips, or exercises, go a long way, especially when conveyed by employees from different roles and tenures. Allow current employees to discuss what they like about working in the company and describe what it is like to work there. Ask them to think about examples of when someone is living a value. Paint a realistic picture—for example, if one of the values is social responsibility, introduce examples of employees in the company's community outreach activities.

RESOURCE

Television and film director Vern Oakley outlines tips for creating videos for new hires in the 2017 *TD* magazine article "How to Direct Great Onboarding Videos."

Gail Griswold gives an example of a company that revamped its onboarding program to communicate its culture with a simulated reality television show in the *TD* magazine article "Making New Hires the Star of the Show—Workplace Rx."

High-level organizational charts allow new or new-to-role employees to pinpoint their place and relationship within the larger business; they also set the stage to present another perspective of the business (Figure 4-1). Introduce processes and reporting relationships (that is, functional, matrix, or dotted lines) and their rationale to give a sense of how the business works. You can also use organizational charts to identify key internal and external stakeholders and place them in the context of the organization. Include photos to make connections between faces and roles easier.

Figure 4-1. Sample Organizational Chart

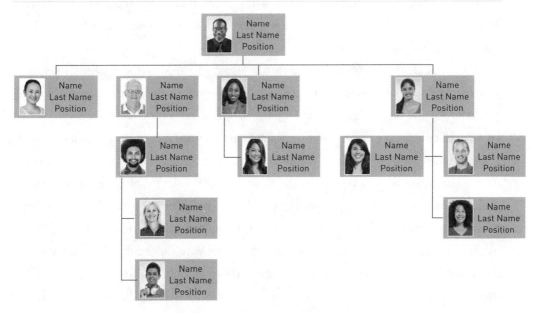

As employees become familiar with the company's key internal and external stakeholders, they also need to grasp the differences between and interactions among production and service areas. Understanding who provides support to whom and who is ultimately accountable to whom will help guide employees to see their roles and potential contributions to the bigger picture in more general terms.

The company's leadership culture and how decisions are made is a natural follow-up topic to the general introduction. Leadership styles, chains of command, preferred ways of address, expected levels of formality, and expectations when interacting with members of different departments or levels are some recommended topics for discussion. Likewise, sharing what to expect from a leader and what it takes to be one in the company can be an aspirational message to new or new-to-role employees. Sharing stories about leaders' paths, especially reinforcing the value of relationships and networks, reinforces the available career opportunities within the company that are so important for employee engagement.

Consider using printed or online reference materials as a way to deliver information. Focus presentations on content that can make an impact on the audience and give participants alternative outlets to learn more about specific topics of interest, such as job aids and portals. Reinforce critical messages through exercises, keeping in mind the organization's culture while designing them. For example, a company built around customer service across all departments can include role plays or simulations about customer service, such as having some employees play employees and others the parts of customers or internal clients.

Facilitators are the face of your onboarding program; therefore, they must be chosen wisely. Assess their subject matter expertise, business knowledge, people skills, and ability to promote learning. Facilitators have to be able to make even the shiest participants feel comfortable and welcome in a new and sometimes intimidating environment; they also have to live the brand. Select facilitators who have the critical competencies outlined in Table 4-2 so that they can leave a lasting positive impression on program attendees.

Table 4-2. Suggested Competencies for Program Facilitators

Competency	Purpose
Use of Core Learning Methods	• Lead large and small groups • Handle participant questions
Time Management	• Adapt to group needs • Keep the group focused and on task
Create Environment Conducive to Learning	• Maintain participant involvement • Ensure participants are comfortable in their surroundings • Focus participant attention on the program instead of venue details such as temperature or table size
Evoke Participation	• Draw attendees into participating actively • Foster openness among participants • Recognize the value of everyone's input
Maintain Objectivity	• Promote balance in participation • Keep emotions under control
Reading Group Dynamics	• Interpret group silence • Clarify uncertainty • Defuse negativity • Discourage arguing and side conversations • Handle conflict positively
Flexibility	• Adapt to the group's needs within the program's design • Redirect the group to the program's topic without coming across as authoritarian

Consistency in the delivery of that branding message is critical to fostering an understanding of the brand, what it stands for, and its importance inside and outside the company. Think of the entire onboarding process as a continuum in the introduction and reinforcement of the company's brand. Every contact with the employee is an opportunity to introduce or reinforce the message. The alignment of the materials' look and feel, logo, types of activities and exercises, layout of space, office decor, employees' personal appearance, facilities' maintenance, and employees' personal warmth convey the right brand message.

PRO TIP

If your company has appropriate spaces to hold these group onboarding sessions on its premises, showcase them among the resources available to employees and to reinforce your company's brand.

Some of the content of the general onboarding program may have to be tailored to meet the logistical needs of remote employees. However, we recommend making participation mandatory whenever business needs allow it, whether in person or by videoconferencing. These general sessions may be one of the few opportunities for the employee to interact directly with other employees from all levels and experience the company's culture firsthand.

Role-Specific Onboarding

The main facilitator in the onboarded employee's role-specific onboarding is the manager, creating a welcoming and engaging environment and ensuring that the employee is connected with colleagues. Similarly, the manager prepares those key stakeholders with whom the new or new-to-role employee will interact often, as well as with those whose functions are interdependent. Further, managers provide feedback and coaching to the onboarded employee through the entire process.

The manager should partner with L&D to design an individualized program focused on role understanding and any specific training needed to perform the role effectively using a variety of learning approaches. For example, a financial analyst will need to become acquainted with the software used and could shadow another analyst to see how to complete common transactions before beginning to execute them in the system. Some of these training needs may be identified during the recruitment and

selection process, while others are standard requirements of the position as sta
job description. Others may be compliance related, and still others may be con
requirements.

The manager or HR could also assign a buddy for the onboarded employee
from their new group of peers. Buddies can offer advice and guidance about day-to-
day operations, provide information, and
ease the onboarded employee's integration into the department and the company through informal interactions for the
first 30 to 60 days. Typically, buddies
have a natural tendency to ease the way
for onboarded employees; however, they
are not mentors, coaches, or employee
managers and should not act as such. At

TOOL

Use the "Buddy Competency Selection
Checklist," located at the end of this
chapter, to determine if your candidates
are suitable for the role of buddy.

the very least, buddies provide companionship during lunch and breaks, and facilitate connections with other employees within and outside the department.

RESOURCE

The human resources support company SaplingHR's "The Free Buddy Program
Playbook" (2017) provides an example of what a buddy program is and should contain.

Program Content for Role-Specific Onboarding

Content for role-specific onboarding must be tailored to meet individual employee
and role needs. Job descriptions are the starting point to plan this content. If the job
descriptions are not up-to-date, ask managers or supervisors to provide insights about
the positions so you can understand the complexities of each and the needs of employees who hold them. Similarly, supervisors and managers can provide information about
potential career paths for those positions, as well as some basics about general development programs. Job descriptions, together with learning needs identified during the
interview process and pre-onboarding, are the foundation for the onboarded employee's individual development plan.

Role-specific onboarding for new employees who have previous experience in your company's industry should focus on company branding and differentiation. In contrast, those who do not have experience in your company's industry (for example, moving from banking to marketing), need to learn about the industry and the business from a very basic level.

New employees who have role-specific experience (such as salespeople), whether it was in your industry or not, need to target differences of the role and culture-specific issues in the company (such as midmarket versus upscale women's retail clothing). Those who do not have previous role experience (perhaps they have never worked in sales), need to go through an intensive program to understand their role in the company's context.

Based on the position's job description and the onboarded employee's background, the manager should create an agenda of meetings, events, and training sessions for the onboarded employee, and suggest points for discussion during those meetings. Managers provide tools and checklists to monitor progress throughout the role-specific onboarding and serve as a clearinghouse for information and resources for onboarded employees.

We have organized role-specific content by themes to pave the way for a smooth delivery; company-specific supporting materials could be made available to employees on the company's intranet or on apps. When preparing videos, make sure they explain how the company's vision emerged, the solutions it provides for customer problems, the company's positive and engaging work environment, and ways employees can grow and develop.

Businesses that do not have these resources available or employees who do not have access to them could receive printed versions of relevant documents and job aids.

That first day of the role-specific onboarding program marks the onboarded employee's transition into their department or unit. After greeting and welcoming them to the department or unit, the manager should meet with the employee to review the agenda for the remainder of the process.

The first point of business is to set the context for the position and clarify role expectations and goals in writing with the onboarded employee; role clarity is crucial for job satisfaction from the first day. Some topics that need to be discussed during that first meeting are:

TOOL

Use the "Simple Onboarding Agenda Sample," located at the end of this chapter, to start planning your role-specific onboarding programs.

- performance expectations
- performance evaluations (that is, when, how, and who performs them)
- supervisor's working style, availability, and communications preferences
- employee's working style, availability, and communications preferences.

Managers should address the department's business plans and goals in face-to-face meetings, whether conducted in person or using virtual meeting technology, and point employees to additional resources such as documents in the company's intranet and other repositories. Company policies and practices as well as workplace culture at the unit level must be part of the overview.

A more detailed description of the department would go beyond organizational charts and include information on department size, reporting structure, roles and functions, products and services, clients and their needs, task distribution, current projects, cyclical projects, collaboration, interdependencies with other departments and units, common acronyms, internal brand, and relationship with corporate. Then include information such as the department's reason for being, core processes, and unique contribution to the business in terms of products, services, and financials.

Present a realistic picture of a typical day in the department or unit from the perspective of the manager and the team, with real-life examples of the department's vision, mission, and values and their connection with those of the overall company. Short testimonial videos could be available in the company's intranet to help employees to connect with their peers. Detail how the department gets things done, its traditions and celebrations (monthly birthday celebrations, recognitions for years of service, holidays), communication preferences (texts for urgent matters, emails for

PRO TIP

Consistently appeal to what drives the onboarded employee to become engaged based on information gathered during the interview process.

what can wait, no voicemails), the meaning of open or closed doors or signs on cubicles, special interest groups and activities customary for the department or unit, and informal interactions within and outside regular working hours. Lastly, explain administrative issues such as dress code, scheduling, job flexibility, and emergency response procedures.

Address diversity issues as they relate most to the role and to the onboarded employee whether or not the onboarded employee attended the general orientation.

Each company has its own definition of diversity and its own idea of what diversity means in its work.

Describe how and when to interact with others at different levels in the organization, how much latitude employees have to go to their supervisors with questions, and how open other leaders are to meeting with employees for whom they do not have direct responsibilities. This is the time to address when to escalate issues, what to do when the employee's supervisor is not available, how open the organization is to the initiative of employees to assume leadership roles, and how much titles and positions really matter in the company.

RESOURCE

In the *TD* magazine article "The Employee Integration Equation," Keith Ferrazzi and Tim Davis (2015) discuss the data showing how critical the first six months of a new hire's employment are. To be successful, an onboarding strategy must be of longer duration and more employee centered.

In this process, new or new-to-role employees should be able to clarify further their roles in the organization and what they are expected to do and not do to advance their careers. It is another way to tackle how much employees can drive their development without overstepping boundaries. Tuition-assistance programs, tuition-reimbursement programs, specialized trainings and courses, and certifications and licenses are some examples. Introduce opportunities for cross-training as well as special projects and assignments in which the onboarded employee could participate.

The program duration of role-specific onboarding will be highly related to the complexity of the role. Avoid information overload at all costs; spread out the content over time and intersperse individual meetings, group meetings, and role-specific training for variety. For example, start and end each day with individual check-in meetings with the supervisor during the first week. Schedule individual meetings over the course of several weeks. Allow time between face-to-face and online training for other activities.

PRO TIP

You can involve your stakeholders in onboarding and make them accountable by allocating onboarding costs to each department's budget.

Consider creating content related to the topics mentioned previously in the company's intranet with titles such as "Knowing Our Department," "Knowing Our Department's History," "A Day in the Life of Our Department," "Knowing How We Work," "Knowing What to Do," "Diversity in Our Department," "Knowing Our Leadership Culture," and "Owning Your Development," so employees can review specific content. Keep it up-to-date.

Role-Specific Onboarding for Managers

L&D faces higher stakes with role-specific onboarding for managers because managers will go on to influence groups of employees whether or not they are direct reports. Factors such as previous experience in the role, company, industry, or elsewhere, as well as tenure in the company when the manager is new to the role, have to be carefully weighed when deciding on the specific components for each manager's role-specific onboarding and their relative importance. Any areas where the onboarded manager lacks experience will demand more intensive attention.

Let's meet Phyllis.

Phyllis's Story

Phyllis is a store manager for Makeup-for-all-of-Us. She has been tasked with onboarding Luigi, who was the last salesperson to join her team before the busy holiday shopping season. Phyllis became a store manager approximately three months ago, but she was never onboarded, and this is her first experience as a manager. She previously served as purchasing supervisor for the company at their main office.

Given this situation, Makeup-for-all-of-Us decided to have Luigi participate in the onboarding program at another store. The manager of that store has been with the company for three years and a top performer for the last two. Phyllis was invited to observe Luigi's onboarding so that she could replicate the process with other employees in the future.

What a great start for Luigi and Phyllis!

Many organizations assume that, because someone has performed a management role in the past, they know what it takes to perform that role in a new context. Overlooking the uniqueness of the new role in the context of the organization can be a costly mistake. Beyond undergoing their own onboarding process, the onboarded managers will also have to transition the team that they inherit and establish themselves as the new leader. This situation is particularly challenging under conditions of organizational restructuring or reorganizations.

Internal role changes, particularly those entailing promotions into managerial roles, entail a separate set of issues. In Phyllis's case, a former peer is becoming a supervisor, which requires additional support from her new manager, her mentor, L&D, and HR. The onboarded manager needs to learn how to redefine relationship boundaries with former peers. This can be challenging, especially if she was close with her former peers, because they might feel excluded when she is handling confidential information and other situations that can only be shared with her new peers and above. In addition, she will have to maintain equity and objectivity at all times and avoid giving any impression of preferential treatment to her former peers.

RESOURCE

In her book *Manager Onboarding: Five Steps for Setting New Leaders Up for Success,* Sharlyn Lauby (2016) focuses on the importance of designing an onboarding program specifically for managers to get started on the path to success instead of waiting for an incident, such as a layoff, a reorganization, or even death, to react and provide training. Such a proactive approach is particularly valuable for new managers whose circumstances change radically after being promoted from within.

The onboarded manager's manager will have to address any decisions to hire externally instead of promoting internally individually with those who applied for or believed they were entitled to the position. Selecting one internal candidate over another may result in emotional reactions from those who were not promoted, especially if the chosen person then becomes the supervisor or manager of those individuals. When an internal promotion occurs, other managers in the company will also require attention during the transition (even if they participated in the promotion decision), because they will need to begin seeing the new manager as their peer. Therefore, the onboarded manager's manager should work with HR and L&D to clarify expectations about that fine line that exists between employee and supervisor among the onboarded manager, their former peers, and their new peers, who will now become their reference group.

Whether the onboarded manager is a new or a new-to-role employee, their manager will also address any challenges related to the business and the internal dynamics of the direct reports during role-specific onboarding. How the position became available (in the case of a new employee) and the management style of the former manager should also be topics of discussion because, unavoidably, the new manager will be compared with the former one. Raising these issues with the onboarded manager will also be relevant because of the shift in relationships (from direct report to peer), subsequent changes in perspective, and access to information.

The type of training and its duration will depend on the onboarded manager's level of experience and background. Another consideration is company expectations for future development, in the case of high-potential employees who were hired to track to senior management roles. Depending on the complexity of the role and company, new managers may participate in local and corporate training.

Many of the onboarded manager's learning experiences will take place during interactions across the organization, which will be critical for current and future roles. For example, senior management will gauge their potential to join their ranks in the future. To facilitate these interactions, the onboarded manager's manager should select and assign a mentor with at least three years of experience in the role and in the company to support the manager for about three months. The mentor will be the new manager's guide to understanding unwritten business rules that include official and nonofficial chains of command, expected work hours, allowed risk taking, relationship building, and social events. The mentor will also provide support in terms of influence, execution, conflict management, recognition, and values, and will become an early warning system to reduce risks that could harm the onboarded manager's career.

TOOL

Use the "Mentor Competency Selection Checklist," located at the end of this chapter, to determine if your candidates are suitable for the role.

By the end of the first week on the job, new managers should at a minimum begin to schedule individual meetings with their direct reports, followed by the rest of the team.

Role-Specific Onboarding for Executives

Based on our experience, companies tend to believe that executives do not need onboarding because they are ready for their roles or they would be ashamed if they are asked to participate in onboarding. Therefore, executive onboarding is a topic that's not addressed, even though unsuccessful executive onboarding has an average cost of 30 percent of an employee's annual salary, according to the U.S. Department of Labor (Fatemi 2016). Further, according to a study from the Center for Creative Leadership, "estimates of outright failure in the first 18 months range from 38 percent to over half, and many more executives fail to be as successful as was predicted in the hiring or promotion phase" (Riddle 2016). An HR in Asia article by Nurlita (2017), referring to the same study, argues that the answer to this problem lies in its onboarding program. Therefore, executives, like all employees, benefit from a structured onboarding program even if the program and key players are different.

RESOURCE

In the *Harvard Business Review* article "Onboarding Isn't Enough," Mark Byford, Michael D. Watkins, and Lena Triantogiannis (2017) provide solid arguments in support of executive onboarding. Cheryl Ndunguru's *The Public Manager* article "Executive Onboarding: How to Hit the Ground Running" (2012), focuses on what organizations can do to reduce the likelihood of executive failure in the federal government. Her insights can be adapted to nongovernment organizations.

The vice president or director of HR usually handles all matters related to executive onboarding off-site to maintain confidentiality, especially when the incoming executive is an external hire who was likely recruited through an external headhunting firm. Often the incoming executive begins onboarding before the current one leaves or even knows they will leave. By the time the incoming executive arrives in the office, they have to be fully knowledgeable about the business and its culture and ready to deliver business results immediately. Other company executives and groups, such as boards of directors, work with the incoming executive to complete a customized development plan using a combination of delivery methods and resources, such as leadership tools, key stakeholder meetings, new leader-team integration events, executive networking forums, and 360-degree assessments and simulations. The goal of these activities is to:

- Ensure the executive's cultural fit in the company.
- Build relationships with other executives.
- Provide political savviness and guidance about unwritten rules.
- Spell out workplace terms and conditions.

- Inform about organizational structure.
- Assist in building the team.

When the incoming executive is promoted internally as part of a succession plan, their manager will also implement a customized development plan. Depending on the industry and the role, this plan may include experiences such as direct role and technical knowledge transfer, attending meetings, leading projects, taking assignments at other locations, assuming other roles, and attending executive training programs.

The entire role-specific onboarding process for executives, whether external hires or internal promotions, typically lasts between six months and a year.

RESOURCE

Douglas Riddle (2016), in *Executive Integration: Equipping Transitioning Leaders for Success*, provides powerful statistics about the rates of executive success and what companies should do to onboard their executives.

The services of an external executive coach are usually contracted to assist in the incoming executive's highly tailored and customized transition process, whether an external hire or promoted employee, and serve as a sounding board. External executive coaches assist with the integration process into the company culture and emphasize leveraging strengths, managing potential blind spots, stakeholder mapping, and structuring processes. They also raise provocative questions and provide a critical external perspective within a safe environment.

The differences in roles for role-specific onboarding discussed so far pertain to employees, regardless of level, who are at the same location. Onboarding remote employees requires additional adjustments in roles, as introduced in the following section.

TOOL

Use the "Executive Coach Competency and Skills Selection Checklist," located at the end of this chapter, to determine if your candidates are suitable for the role.

Role-Specific Onboarding for Remote Employees

In general, the content for a remote employee's role-specific onboarding is similar to that of anyone else performing the role on-site. However, the onboarded employee has to be held accountable to the same standards as those who have more traditional work arrangements. Buddies or mentors may also be assigned at the local office where the remote employee works, thus gaining additional significance because they can provide information about housing, schools, basic services, and cultural norms. Counterparts at the home office will offer supplementary information and foster that sense of connection with the rest of the team.

PRO TIP

Make sure that at least one co-worker, peer, or direct report of a remote employee sends an email or makes a phone call to connect with the employee and see how they're doing each day; maintaining contact between the remote employee and the rest of the team fosters a sense of belonging.

Role-specific onboarding is also the best time to establish company expectations of the remote employee's participation in events at the main office or the office to which they report. Including the employee in meetings and other business affairs, considering time differences and any other geographical issues, and coming up with creative inclusive ideas for celebrations and other workplace traditions to ensure the remote employee's participation are ways to maintain contact during and after role-specific onboarding.

The challenges of conducting role-specific onboarding for these employees lie in adapting the content and handling the logistics to deliver the content. Nothing substitutes for direct personal contact regardless of group size. Online communication tends to be best for completing forms and some training sessions; it is also the primary training delivery option for remote employees. If your company prefers delivery through online programs, limit the session duration to no more than two hours and a maximum of four hours per day. Use a variety of teaching tools and direct interactions when you design online programs. Tailor the information to the media that you use, keeping in mind the best way to chunk information based on the media's characteristics, such as number of characters or words allowed. Make sure that all information is self-explanatory.

Logistics for Onboarding

When designing onboarding programs, you'll need to make many decisions about the logistics, including venue selection, room temperature, room lighting, sound systems, room setup, refreshments, snacks, meals, parking arrangements, audio-visual equipment, computers for online trainings or transactions, videoconferencing and Internet connectivity or systems access, printed materials, promotional materials, special needs of attendees (for example, ramps, larger fonts, or dietary restrictions), and special accommodations (such as security staff for certain members of top management). Use company facilities and resources as much as possible, considering the number of attendees as well as the types of activities and exercises based on the group's profile. However, if your company lacks the appropriate space, find the right venue and use it regularly; familiarity with the locale and its staff will be beneficial because they will be able to anticipate your needs as a regular client.

Role-specific onboarding takes place mainly at the department or unit level. However, aspects such as reserving rooms for private meetings (particularly in open-office layouts), finding appropriate restaurants for those important "let's get acquainted" lunches, and all other preparations have to be in place before onboarding begins.

Individual meetings need to be coordinated in advance and participants have to be aware of their role. Schedule meetings at the hosts' offices so the onboarded employee can become familiar with the different areas of the business. If the organization is spread among several buildings or locations, schedule several meetings that will take place at the same building for a morning or an afternoon to minimize travel time.

Logistics gain additional salience for role-specific onboarding for remote employees. They'll need to learn how to optimize the technology they'll use to work remotely. The availability of online resources and these employees' time at the headquarters or office to which they report has to be leveraged for the particular learning experiences required. Still, the manager should make special efforts to conduct initial contacts in person to develop the manager-employee relationship.

The manager has to hold group meetings using technology, touch base with the employee personally during business trips, and convene the entire team to interact directly on a regular basis, also relying mostly on technology.

Communicating About New Arrivals

Preparations for the arrival of the new employee include setting in motion a series of activities that require the participation of different departments. Be advised that some appointments or business situations, such as replacements at the executive level, may require maintaining higher levels of confidentiality and discretion.

PRO TIP

Communicate the arrival of every new or new-to-role employee across the organization. Personalization matters!

Sharing the news about a new or new-to-role employee is more effective when you've planned the process out in advance. It's also helpful to use different media for the announcements; for example, some companies have electronic bulletin boards while others use a more traditional format such as posters.

A cascade model is best used when managers are the first to know about the new employee, possibly because they participated in the selection process. The next communication layer should be the department the onboarded employee is joining; that group should receive the news before the rest of the organization. Make sure the manager communicates the new employee's starting date, position, and background, as well as how they will be an asset for the team and for the business.

TOOL

Use the "Sample Email Announcement," located at the end of the chapter, to communicate the arrival of a new employee to the organization.

After that meeting, have the manager write an organization-wide announcement for HR to release using the customary means, ranging from printed to electronic communication, as well as updates to relevant directories. The announcement should include who is joining the company, the position or role, general background information, and some details of what you would like others to know about the person. Keep it short, simple, and memorable; stay away from flowery language, jargon, and longwinded biographical sketches. Remember that everyone in the organization will receive this information. Prepare a more detailed bio of no more than 75 words to post on the intranet or for specific groups.

PRO TIP

Create a new-hire webpage or tab in your company's intranet with useful information for the new employee, such as nearby services like ATMs, transportation alternatives, childcare, and food delivery.

Understanding the Timing of Implementation

Implementing the onboarding program is as important as designing it. Onboarding consists of pre-onboarding, general onboarding, and role-specific onboarding. Each one of these components has its own timing and contributors. Strategically articulating each one's contributions will make a difference in the employee's experience, which must be tailored according to their role in the company. In the next chapter, we will discuss what you need to do to gather data to evaluate your program.

Questions to Explore

- What will you do to ensure the support of the other departments for the onboarding program?
- What program components have you considered for your onboarding program?
- Does the company see the value of pre-onboarding? If not, what will you do to influence key stakeholders?
- How do the materials that your company provides to new employees reflect the company's brand? What can you do to improve them?
- Have you built progress and logistical checkpoints in your company's onboarding program?
- How does your company communicate the arrival of a new employee? What can be done differently?
- What topics do you include in your company's new employee orientation? What don't you include? Why?
- What competencies do you look for in your onboarding facilitators?

- How do managers participate in your company's role-specific onboarding?
- How do your company's employees respond to having a buddy or mentor?
- What is the main driver of employee engagement among your company's new employees?
- How is role-specific onboarding different for individual contributors, managers, executives, and remote employees? How is it similar?
- How does your company customize the content of its role-specific onboarding for each position?
- How will you convince managers, who are already overwhelmed with work, of the importance of role-specific onboarding and their responsibility in its success?
- If you were your company's owner, what would you like the onboarding program to include?

Tools for Support

Department Support Checklist

Use this checklist to track the status of what you need from other company departments for onboarding programs.

Department	Task	Status
Information Systems	Grant access to systems	
	Assign computer	
	Assign telephone extension	
	Assign cellular telephone	
	Create email account	
	Create other media accounts	
Security or HR	Issue identification card	
	Issue key card access	
Personnel/Payroll	Receive payroll processing and payment information	
Facilities	Assign workspace	
	Prepare workspace	
	Assign lockers/storage	
	Reserve parking space	
	Grant parking access	
Human Resources	Obtain uniforms (if required)	
	Obtain specialized tools and equipment	
	Obtain individualized materials for the workspace	
	Request business cards	
	Assign company vehicles	
	Handle relocation	

Onboarding Checklist

Use this checklist to go through the entire onboarding process. It details what you need to do and the topics you need to discuss.

Employee Name:		Date:	
Department:		Manager:	
Action	**Status**	**Responsible**	**Comments**
Prior to Employee Arrival			
Prepare departmental welcome packet: job description, contact names, and phone/email list			
Review employee area/space/cubicle			
Identify computer needs and requirements, and arrange for access to company network and systems			
Arrange phone extension, mobile phone, or peripherals			
Establish reviewed goals and objectives			
Identify a buddy			
Meet with the buddy to establish plan and share thoughts and tips			
Prepare the calendar for the first week			
Set up meetings with other departments or critical people			
Arrange facilities tour			
Arrange or enroll in any required training sessions			
Review employee handbook and policies (be ready for questions)			
Review department organizational chart			
Activate the internal security processes			
Review employee training schedule with L&D			
Coordinate with HR about announcement email			
The Day Before the Employee Starts			
Call employee and confirm start date, time, place, dress code, and parking			
Email (refresh) department of the new hire			

Action	Status	Responsible	Comments
First Day With Manager			
Greet the employee			
Introduce the employee to others			
Discuss the employee's orientation			
Share department mission and goals			
Discuss department's customers and who supports the department			
Discuss job description; outline responsibilities, goals, and objectives			
Share first week schedule			
Provide a departmental overview			
Review policies and procedures as they pertain to your department (attendance, overtime, flexible hours, confidentiality, breaks, and meals)			
Take employee to lunch			
Assist the employee in accessing company system, intranet, and emails			
First Week			
Assign a shadow (colleague) in the department [optional]			
Walk through the employee onboarding portal (if available)			
Review training schedule with employee			
Discuss on-the-job-training plan			
Review technology functionality			
Explain the performance review			
Ask for first week feedback			
Answer any questions			
Meet with colleagues to discuss their perceptions			
First Month			
Expected results: Employees are aware of what is expected from their position. Building relationships, acquiring skills, and learning competencies.			
Conduct 30-day performance review			
Review short- and long-term goals			
Ask for 30-day feedback			
Answer questions			
Have a check-in with employee buddy			
Take employee to lunch			

Action	Status	Responsible	Comments
Meet with employee and buddy to review first weeks			
Continue introducing employee to key people			
Ensure employee has attended scheduled training			
Confirm that employee registered for scheduled training			
Next 60 Days			
Expected results: Employees are knowledgeable of their position. Require less supervision, and continue acquiring skills, competencies, and company know-how.			
Conduct performance review			
Review short- and long-term goals			
Ask for feedback			
Answer questions			
Have a check-in with employee buddy			
Ensure employee attended required training sessions			
Have a monthly check-in with the employee and buddy			
Create opportunity for employee to attend or be involved in activities outside the department			
One Year Review			
Expected Results: Employees are performing and meeting expectations.			
Conduct a yearly performance review			
Discuss setbacks or worries			
Answer any questions			
Request feedback about role, department, and company as a whole			
Discuss goals for next year			

Suggested Contents for Welcome Packet

The following items are helpful to include in the new employee welcome packet:

- Welcome letter and HR documents
- Map of the company
- Handouts, policies, and procedures for review and acknowledgment
- General benefits information
- Marketing materials
- Reference to company's websites and links
- Company contact list
- Dates to remember
- Contact information for the help desk and other support (if applicable)

Sample Email Communication With Employee to Be Onboarded

The following is an example of an email to send to new employees once they're hired, but before their first day.

Subject: Next Week's Onboarding Information

Christine,

We are glad to welcome you to the office next week! Here is everything that you need to know about employee onboarding at IR Sound Corp.

Your First Day and How to Find the Office
When you arrive on Wednesday (please come in around 9:30 a.m.), I will be there to get you settled. We'll get started with your onboarding and I will introduce you to some basics about our business. You will begin to get to know our global team (yes, we are global, we have offices in Los Angeles, Las Vegas, Puerto Rico, and London), how we communicate, our systems, and our sound technology. Following are some details about how to find our main office.

[Insert map and directions or drop a pin]

Let's Get Started
When you come in on Wednesday, you will find your computer ready. You will receive your username and a temporary password so that you can get set up following our security checklist. Your ID is ready for you in the security office.

Office Practices
We usually wear casual clothes in the office, so feel free to wear sneakers. Your company polos with our logo will arrive in a week.

We try to have lunch together as a team in our fully equipped lunchroom around 1-1:30 p.m.; there are snacks around the office in case you get hungry before then. You may bring your own food or get carryout from one of the nearby eateries.

You and I will have coffee at 3 p.m. at the IR Cafe. The team also wants to take you out for dinner on Wednesday night! Look for a calendar invite from Leo for details.

Meeting the Team

You will meet the team on Wednesday at 10:30 a.m. You'll also have onboarding meetings with team leads during the rest of your first week. Of course, you will spend quite some time with **[Name of direct supervisor].**

Please let me know if you have any questions before then! Feel free to call, text, or WhatsApp me at 123-345-5678.

Welcome!
Iván

Onboarding and Engagement Manager

Buddy Competency Selection Checklist

Use this checklist to determine if your candidates will work well as buddies.

Name:			New Employee's Name:
Completed by:			Date:
Selection Criteria	Yes	No	Comments
Knowledge of the Business			
Contacts Across Organization			
Role-Specific Knowledge			
Knowledge of Dos and Don'ts of Unit			
Commitment to Knowledge Transfer			
Interpersonal Skills			
Communication Skills			
Listening Skills			
Availability to Answer Questions			
Genuine Desire to Help			
Resource for Unwritten Rules			
Role Knowledge			
Role Model			
Strong Performer			
Patient			
Accessibility			

Simple Onboarding Agenda Sample

Use this sample agenda to start planning your role-specific onboarding programs.

Day 1

Activity	Schedule
Welcome by manager	8 a.m.
Overview of the day	8:30-9 a.m.
Knowing our department	9-10 a.m.
Tour of the department or unit and introduction to team	10-11:30 a.m.
Getting acquainted with your office	11:30 a.m.-12:30 p.m.
Lunch with manager	12:30-1:30 p.m.
Role expectations and goals	1:30-3 p.m.
Time at your desk	3-4:45 p.m.
Closing and feedback of first day with manager	4:45-5 p.m.

Day 2

Activity	Schedule
Welcome by manager	8 a.m.
Check-in with new employee about the first day	8:15-8:45 a.m.
A day in the life with the team: knowing how we work	8:45-9:45 a.m.
Time at your desk	9:45 a.m.-12:30 p.m.
Lunch with the team	12:30-2 p.m.
Online training: XXX System	2-4 p.m.
Informal interaction with mentor or buddy	4-4:30 p.m.
Closing and feedback of second day with manager	4:30-4:45 p.m.

Day 3

Activity	Schedule
Welcome by manager	8 a.m.
Check-in with new employee about the second day	8:30-9 a.m.
Around the office: Meet key people in your department	9-10:30 a.m.
Knowing your mentor or buddy	10:30-11:15 a.m.
Time at your desk	11:15 a.m.-12:30 p.m.
Lunch with your mentor or buddy	12:30-1:30 p.m.
Buddy: Planning for the second week and beyond	1:30-2 p.m.
Shadow a peer to learn best practices	2-3:30 p.m.
Read product guides	3:30-4:45 p.m.
Closing and feedback of third day with manager	4:45-5 p.m.

Mentor Competency Selection Checklist

Use this checklist to help you determine if your candidates will be suitable mentors.

Name:			New Employee's Name:
Completed by:			Date:
Selection Criteria	Yes	No	Comments
Self-Aware			
Understands Others			
Strong Communication Skills			
Active Listener			
Effective Questioning			
Works Cross-Culturally			
Builds Trust			
Business Savvy			
Politically Experienced			
Role Model			
Available Online and Face-to-Face			
Lives the Brand			
Resource for Information About Workplace Culture and Norms			
High Performance			
Strong Interpersonal Skills			
Resourceful			

Executive Coach Competency and Skills Selection Checklist

Use this checklist to determine if your candidates are suitable for the role of executive coach.

Name:		
Selection Criteria	Yes	No
Communicator		
Good at Questioning		
Trustworthy		
Maintains Confidentiality		
Manages Stress		
Knowledgeable About Team Building		
Accessible		
Active Listener		
Experienced		
Objective		
Certified		
Previous Executive Coaching Experience		

Sample Email Announcement

Use a version of this sample email to share a new employee's arrival and contact information.

To: All Employees
Cc:
Bcc:
Subject: Welcoming Ana Irma Smith

I'm very pleased to announce that Ana Smith will be joining us as diversity and inclusion manager on **[date]**.

Ana will be responsible for all diversity and inclusion initiatives, strategies, and programs. Diversity and inclusion are integral to the excellence and success of our association, but they are especially vital for the strength of our goals. **[Include information about what people need to know.]**

Please come to **[location]** to meet Ana and welcome her to our team.

You can reach Ana at:
◊ **[office location]**
◊ **[office number or ext.]**
◊ **[mobile number]**
◊ **[email address]**
◊ **[intranet code]**
◊ **[Skype code]**

Best Regards,

[Name of Manager]

Additional Resources

AON. 2017. *2017 Trends in Global Engagement.* www.aon.com/engagement17.

ATD Staff. 2015. "Making New Hires the Star of the Show." *TD*, May. www.td.org /magazines/td-magazine/making-new-hires-the-star-of-the-show.

Bevegni, S.H. 2015. *Kit de incorporación de personal.* Linkedin Talent Solutions, October 1. https://business.linkedin.com/content/dam/business/talent-solutions/regional /es-es/c/pdfs/Onboarding-in-a-Box_ES_FORMS_FINAL.pdf.

Biech, E. 2017. *The Art and Science of Training.* Alexandria, VA: ATD Press.

Byford, M., M.D. Watkins, and L. Triantogiannis. 2017. "Onboarding Isn't Enough." *Harvard Business Review*, May-June.

Chanel. 2013. "Coco–Inside Chanel." September 12. www.youtube.com/watch?v= 2G88zqPxJ00.

Crebar, A. 2018. "Top 7 Employee Onboarding Programs." Sapling, April 15. www .trysapling.com/resources/top-7-employee-onboarding-programs.

Dávila, N., and W. Piña-Ramírez. 2013. *Cutting Through the Noise: The Right Employee Engagement Strategies for You.* Alexandria, VA: ASTD Press.

DGS (Delta Global Staffing). 2016. *Associate Onboarding Manual: Everything You Need to Know.* July 15. http://deltaglobalstaffing.com/images/pdfs/dgs-associate-a1 -onboarding-manual-01.pdf.

Fatemi, F. 2016. "The True Cost of a Bad Hire—It's More Than You Think." *Forbes*, September 28. www.forbes.com/sites/falonfatemi/2016/09/28/the-true-cost -of-a-bad-hire-its-more-than-you-think/#3152d2454aa4.

Ferrazzi, K., and T. Davis. 2015. "The Employee Integration Equation." *TD* 69(10): 57-60. www.td.org/magazines/td-magazine/the-employee-integration-equation.

KPMG. 2017. "New Director Onboarding." KPMG Board Leadership Center, September 24. https://boardleadership.kpmg.us/boardroom-resources/resources -directors/new-director-onboarding.html.

Lauby, S. 2016. *Manager Onboarding: Five Steps for Setting New Leaders Up for Success.* Alexandria, VA: SHRM Press.

Locke, E., and Associates. 2014. "Onboarding Coaching." Ellis Locke & Associates, February 24. http://ellislocke.com/services/coaching/onboarding-coaching.

Lynn University Employee Services. 2011. "New Employee Onboarding Program." Lynn University, June 9. https://my.lynn.edu/ICS/icsfs/Onboarding_Process .pdf?target=9ee8e458-a8d8-4ada-a874-17190a5dd1e9.

Martin, M. 2010. "Set Up an Efficient Onboarding Process for New Employees." Dummies, May 10. www.dummies.com/business/human-resources/employee-engagement/set-up-an-efficient-onboarding-process-for-new-employees.

Meirest, D. 2016. "Game On: Don't Leave Your Onboarding Success to Chance." *HR Magazine* 60(15): 104-107.

Ndunguru, C. 2012. "Executive Onboarding: How to Hit the Ground Running." *The Public Manager*, Fall. www.td.org/magazines/the-public-manager/executive -onboarding-how-to-hit-the-ground-running.

Nurlita. 2017. "Onboarding Senior Leadership: Things to Consider for HR Managers." HR in Asia, April 14. www.hrinasia.com/recruitment/onboarding-senior-leadership -things-to-consider-for-hr-managers.

Oakley, V. 2017. "How to Direct Great Onboarding Videos." *TD* 71(9): 26-29.

Padgett Powers, M. 2016. "Power Switch: Onboarding Tips From the Experts Who Help New Presidents Fill 4,000-Plus Positions in Less Than 90 Days." *HR Magazine* 61(7): 60-66.

Pennsylvania State Human Resources Office. 2014. *HR Office's Onboarding Handbook.* HR Service Center, May 21. www.hrm.oa.pa.gov/hire-sep/Hiring/Documents /onboarding-handbook-hr.pdf

Riddle, D. 2016. *Executive Integration: Equipping Transitioning Leaders for Success.* Center for Creative Leadership whitepaper. www.ccl.org/wp-content/uploads/2015/04 /ExecutiveIntegration.pdf

Sapling HR. 2017. "Free Buddy Program Playbook." Sapling Google Doc. https:// docs.google.com/document/d/1ICBxJ7wJV523BYw4uqlD4_wQBlRhNP6W W2JuLK6dkv8/edit.

Slavov, N. 2014. "The History of Nike—Brand Evolution." November 19. www.youtube .com/watch?v=MQNgJ2mpW9I.

U.S. Office of Personnel Management. 2011. *Hit the Ground Running: Establishing a Model Executive Onboarding Program.* OPM, October 1. www.opm.gov/WIKI/uploads /docs/Wiki/OPM/training/Hit_the_Ground_Running_Establishing_a_Model _Executive_Onboarding_Framework_2011.pdf.

Valve. 2012. *Valve Handbook for New Employees: A Fearless Adventure in Knowing What to Do When No One's There Telling You What to Do.* Bellevue, WA: Valve Press. www.valvesoftware.com/company/Valve_Handbook_LowRes.pdf.

Vargas, J. 2013. "Generation Y Yearns for Challenging and Satisfying Government Work." *TD* 67(3): 58-62.

Westwood, R., and L. Johnson. 2011. "Onboarding for Managers." *Infoline.* Alexandria, VA: ASTD Press.

Zenefits. 2016. "The Definitive Guide to Onboarding: The First 30 Days." Zenefits, March 17. www.zenefits.com/get/ultimate-onboarding-guide.

5

Transferring Learning and Evaluating Results: How Do You Demonstrate Success?

In This Chapter

- Value of measurement and evaluation in onboarding
- Understanding metrics, measurement, and evaluation
- Benefits of evaluating onboarding programs
- Communicating results

An onboarding program's implementation is not complete without a measurement and evaluation component that reflects the Kirkpatrick model for evaluation and the Phillips model for metrics and ROI. Like any business process, onboarding programs require consistent measurement and reporting. However, according to the *2017 Strategic Onboarding Survey Report* by HR Daily Advisor Research, 45 percent of survey participants did not evaluate their onboarding programs. In another study conducted by Kronos and the Human Capital Institute, 55 percent of companies reported that they lacked the tools to measure the effectiveness of their onboarding programs (Filipkowski, Heinsch, and Wiete 2017).

According to Deloitte's *Global Human Capital Trends Study 2015,* only 22 percent of HR professionals have the data, business skill set, and mindset necessary for business success. Deloitte goes further to state that even the most data-knowledgeable HR teams may not be conversant about their company's financial and business strategy, or able to articulate the value of programs, plans, and decisions that they make for employees in business terms.

This book has built a case for how onboarding starts with the recruitment and selection process. Now we'll take you through the evaluation process for your onboarding program. Certainly, the best candidates, whether new to the company or new to the role, call for the best onboarding program that the company can provide to connect and stay connected with them. Thus, onboarding, even though many of its components rely on checklists to ensure task completion, is more than a checklist.

But how is the completion of checklists related to the program's evaluation? How do checklists make a difference? They are one way, among others, for organizations to calculate return on investment, confirm they retain talent, document lower turnover rates, and assess revenue levels as a result of onboarding.

PRO TIP

The best way to link the results of your onboarding program to business results is by establishing relationships between business and HR metrics, such as employee turnover and employee engagement.

Employee engagement is a measure tied to business results that has to be carefully monitored throughout onboarding and afterward. According to Kevin Sheridan (2012) in *Building a Magnetic Culture*, the 10 main drivers for early engagement by new hires are:

- career development
- strategy and mission
- job content
- availability of resources to perform the job effectively
- senior management's relationship with employees
- recognition
- direct supervisor or manager leadership abilities
- open and effective communication
- co-worker satisfaction and cooperation
- organizational culture.

These engagement drivers have all been addressed throughout the onboarding process we have discussed. They will have an impact on employee retention, which is the main company concern after employee selection.

RESOURCE

In *Cutting Through the Noise: The Right Employee Engagement Strategies for You*, we discuss the entire employee engagement process, provide various tools to foster employee engagement, and link engagement to business results (Dávila and Piña-Ramírez 2013).

Here's an example of a missed opportunity for early engagement:

Pandora's Story

Pandora is the human resources generalist in charge of the general onboarding program for a chain of mass-market household goods retail stores. Three years ago, her company selected an off-the-shelf web-based program and customized it to address the company's basic history, mission, vision, and values. Information about employee benefits, general company policies and practices, and the employee handbook are also included in this program, which takes about eight hours to complete. Short videos about the importance of employee engagement are included, but the stories and characters in these videos are not representative of the employee population at the stores.

When Pandora presented the last turnover data report to senior management, some questioned why cashiers were leaving before completing their first year with the company. Their exits cost about $3,000 per cashier in resources such as hiring time, HR staff time, job posting fees, and interviewing time, plus employee time spent on the online program. There were also overtime costs incurred by those cashiers who covered the shifts for new employees who were not yet proficient at their jobs. In addition, employee engagement scores for the cashiers' group were at historically low levels. The district manager said that the problem was that new employees were disappointed because there was no onboarding.

Pandora became defensive, immediately responding that they had an online onboarding program. She placed the blame on managers and supervisors who did not follow up on the program and left cashiers alone to do their work soon after they received training. Senior managers did not agree with Pandora and requested action. They wanted a cost-effective onboarding program that would reduce the time cashiers needed to become proficient at their jobs.

When Pandora reviewed exit interview data she found employee comments about not having the information and tools needed to do their jobs. She also found that employees were not completing the online onboarding process. She knew that this information would not satisfy the senior managers. Instead, she needed to explain the costs of onboarding versus the costs of replacing employees and be proactive about measuring the program's financial impact to get senior managers' attention and support.

The Value of Measurement and Evaluation in Onboarding

Because onboarding continues after employee orientation ends, companies can measure its impact along the way and establish clear connections with employee performance. Let's meet Ylde.

Ylde's Story

Ylde received a disciplinary action after four weeks on the job for not following the company's email policy. Víctor, Ylde's supervisor and the policy writer, indicated that Ylde was using company property for personal purposes during working hours, which was not allowed.

Ylde argued that in his previous job employees were allowed to use company email for some personal purposes. He said that he had not received information about the policy during what he believed was his role-specific onboarding, and he was simply following what everybody else was doing.

Yadira, the human resources generalist assigned to his business unit, confirmed that Víctor had reduced Ylde's onboarding and that Ylde had never signed the employee handbook acknowledgment in the system. Further, Víctor had not given Ylde any role-specific onboarding or met with him except to give him the policy memo.

With the negative impact of such an oversight on the business, companies cannot afford to wait until a disciplinary action comes up to find out that employee onboarding was not conducted properly. Situations such as Ylde's highlight the importance of measuring, tracking, and evaluating onboarding programs.

Some statistics will help clarify the importance of evaluation. According to a report by Talya Bauer for the SHRM Foundation in 2010, more than 25 percent of employees experience career transitions each year, 50 percent of hourly workers leave during their first four months of employment, and 50 percent of senior outside hires fail at their jobs within 18 months. Roy Maurer, writing for SHRM in 2015, reported similar trends. Of about a thousand respondents to a 2014 survey by BambooHR, "[a]bout one third of new hires who had quit said they'd barely had any onboarding or none at all and 15 percent of respondents noted that lack of an effective onboarding program contributed to their decision to quit."

These percentages represent a significant impact on the company's bottom line. But, what should you measure?

In business, what gets measured is what receives attention and is valuable. New employees are an important investment for the future of the company—the average cost per hire is $4,129 (SHRM 2016) and that becomes much higher for executives. In addition, replacement costs can equal as much as twice an employee's annual salary (Maurer 2015). This investment demands a carefully planned measurement and evaluation process. Evaluations also provide information about what worked well and what did not, as well as the perceptions of what is being done to make future onboarding program implementations more effective.

Metrics and evaluation provide the information you need to champion change in your organization, and your findings will demonstrate your company's competitive position, particularly if you compare data from before and after implementing the onboarding program. Most businesses are well served by the metrics they've already collected for other purposes—such as turnover rate, employee retention, and transaction rates—when they evaluate their onboarding programs.

As programs become more linked to business strategy, conversations about why companies invest, how they invest, and what return they get on their investment become part of the day-to-day operations. Numbers say it all. Measure what you can control.

Metrics, Measurement, and Evaluation

In our practice we still find many professionals using the terms *metrics, measurement,* and *evaluation* interchangeably. Let's define what we mean by these terms within the context of evaluating onboarding program results:

- **Metrics** refers to standards of performance and progress, also known as key performance indicators (KPIs), that can be quantified, such as net sales, revenue growth, employee turnover, and recruitment costs.
- **Measurement** pertains to the actual process of assigning value to those metrics, such as calculating onboarding costs, obtaining employee time to productivity, and assigning performance ratings.
- **Evaluation** involves analyzing and making judgments about information obtained through formative (sequentially over a period of time) or summative (at the end of the process or program) measurement.

There are many benefits of measuring and evaluating onboarding programs, including:

- obtaining consistent information to compare over time to track the impact of the program (for example, how long are employees staying with the company)
- quantifying the scope of the challenge and costs to justify current and future investments in onboarding
- collecting a baseline against which to compare progress and sustain buy-in as the business determines how onboarding is affecting its bottom line (for example, reduction in time to productivity)
- comparing the results of your company's program with those of other companies when publicly available (for example, a reduction in the number of accidents and errors)

PRO TIP

When you focus on business outcomes, be sure to consider performance rather than just activity.

- addressing any affirmative action issues as you document profiles of participants across program components
- determining how the program contributes to the business so the company can set priorities
- giving a real sense of the importance of onboarding programs for the business, so that decision makers see its value through data.

RESOURCE

"How to Measure the Return on Your HR Investment: Using ROI to Demonstrate Business Impact" by Jack and Patti Phillips (2002) provides foundation about ROI you can use for your program. This creates a structure to measure results based on a proven approach.

One way to increase management's awareness of the importance of measurement and evaluation is to highlight the actual costs of onboarding programs and the potential costs if they are not done correctly. In addition to the straight costs of onboarding an employee, companies need to look at other hidden costs when considering associated recruitment costs, such as the cost of losing the best candidate for a position due to an inappropriate onboarding program.

PRO TIP

According to a survey from Korn Ferry (2017), 90 percent of responding executives said they believed onboarding programs were key to retaining employees. The majority of those surveyed stated that between 10 and 25 percent of new hires leave within their first six months of employment.

Measures and Indicators

Use a variety of measures and indicators for each onboarding component, such as those shown in Tables 5-1, 5-2, and 5-3. Remember to start with metrics that are already available. If you try to collect every single one, especially if you do so simultaneously, it could be confusing and difficult to sustain.

PRO TIP

Gather feedback from onboarding participants using surveys, interviews, focus groups, follow-up sessions, questionnaires, and on-the-job observations. It is best to collect information from different sources so that you can compare results to identify and track trends.

Table 5-1. Suggested Metrics for Onboarding Programs: Pre-Onboarding

Metrics	What to Collect	Owner
Recruitment Metrics	• Number of applicants • Number of applicants interviewed • Number of offers extended • Number of offers accepted • Time to hire • Time to start	Human Resources
Interview Costs	• Time costs for all participants • Materials, travel, and meal costs (usually for executives or highly specialized job offers)	Human Resources
Testing Costs	• Costs of administering skills, personality, competency, knowledge, and drug tests if applicable	Learning and Development Human Resources
Welcome Packet Costs	• Costs of design, printing, and copies of materials • Costs of promotional materials to reinforce brand	Learning and Development Marketing and Communications
Communications Costs	• Costs of announcement design, printing, display about new or new-to-role employees • Frequently asked questions for staff	Human Resources, Learning and Development, and Communications
Staff Time	• Preparation for pre-onboarding phase according to role • Participation in pre-onboarding phase according to role	Various Departments

Table 5-2. Suggested Metrics for Onboarding Programs: General Onboarding

Metrics	What to Collect	Owner
Orientation Material Costs	• Design, printing, and copies of materials • Promotional materials to reinforce brand	Learning and Development
Computer Room Use	• Rental or use of computer training rooms • Costs of technical support staff	Learning and Development Information Systems
Facilitator's Preparation	• Time for facilitators to review content and get ready for orientation • Costs of training subject matter experts as facilitators	Learning and Development
Facilitator Time	• Time to deliver content and general orientation	Various Departments (including L&D)
Participant Evaluation Forms	• Form design, printing, and tabulation • Design and tabulation in electronic form (if available)	Learning and Development
New Employee Satisfaction	• Survey design and administration in paper or electronic form	Learning and Development
Rate of Compliance With Legal Issues	• Documentation requirements • Time worked reported • Overtime rules • Progressive discipline process • Mandatory training	Human Resources
Retention Rates	• Number of employees who stay after 30, 60, or 90 days, and one year	Human Resources
Turnover Rates	• Number of employees who leave the company after 30, 60, or 90 days, and one year	Human Resources

TOOL

Get participant feedback by adapting the "Evaluation Forms" at the end of this chapter. Use the orientation feedback form to get new and new-to-role employee input about the orientation. After employees have been onboarded, have them fill out onboarding feedback forms at 30 and 90 days.

Table 5-3. Suggested Metrics for Onboarding Programs: Role-Specific Onboarding

Metrics	What to Collect	Owner
Onboarding Costs	• Meetings and special sessions • Role-specific training • Travel • Meals • Team activities • Targeted materials • Workspace set up at the department level	Learning and Development Departments and Units Involved
Time to Productivity vs. Average Tenured Employee	• Amount of time it takes employees to perform at comparable level of those of average tenure	Departments and Units
Check-In With Manager at 30 Days	• Role understanding • Alignment between role and employee expectations • Suggestions to improve onboarding	Learning and Development
Check-In With Manager at 60 Days	• Enablers and barriers for success • Resources that have been the most and least helpful • Ability to meet manager's expectations • Sense of accomplishment	Learning and Development
Check-In With Manager at 90 Days	• Enablers and barriers for success • Resources that have been the most and least helpful • Ability to meet manager's expectations • Sense of accomplishment	Learning and Development
Annual Performance Review	• Results of performance review and evaluation	Managers Human Resources
Employee Engagement	• Engagement results for employees with one year or less of tenure	Learning and Development
Employee Onboarding Satisfaction	• Satisfaction with entire onboarding program, measured either by phase or at the end	Learning and Development
Manager Onboarding Satisfaction	• Satisfaction with entire onboarding program, measured either by phase or at the end	Learning and Development
Customer Satisfaction	• Satisfaction of internal and external customers with services provided by new or new-to-role employee	Learning and Development
Productivity after 30, 60, and 90 days	• Department's indicators of productivity	Department or Unit
Exit Interview	• Information about why employees leave the company	Human Resources
Stay Interviews	• Information about what makes an employee stay in the company	Learning and Development

TOOL

A simple survey, such as the "Sample Onboarding Survey" included at the end of this chapter, can provide useful information without overburdening participants. Include an email to introduce the request to complete the survey.

The following formulas will help you calculate some of the most commonly used metrics to evaluate your onboarding program.

Turnover Rate

The turnover rate tells you how many employees left the company. You need to be alert for any changes in turnover rates because of the cost that turnover represents for the business.

To calculate employee turnover rates, select the timeframe (for example, one year), divide the number of employee separations by the average number of active employees during that timeframe, then multiply by 100.

$$\text{Turnover Rate} = \frac{\text{Number of Employee Separations } (during\ selected\ period\ of\ time)}{\text{Average Number of Employees } (during\ the\ same\ period\ of\ time)} \times 100$$

Retention Rates

The retention rate tells you how many employees stayed in the company.

To calculate the retention rate, which is a percentage, select the end of the timeframe (for example, one year), divide the total number of employees still employed at the start of the time period, then multiply this number by 100.

$$\text{Retention Rate (\%)} = \frac{\text{Total Number of Employees Still Employed at End of Time Period}}{\text{Total Number of Employees at Start of Time Period}} \times 100$$

Average Time to Fill

The average time to fill refers to the ratio between how many days positions are open and the total number of positions open. To calculate the average time to fill, divide the total number of days that positions are open by the total number of positions open.

$$\text{Average Time to Fill} = \frac{\text{Total Number of Days That Positions Are Open}}{\text{Total Number of Positions Open}}$$

Cost per Hire

The cost per hire considers the external and internal costs related to bringing a new employee into the company, to determine the average cost to hire a new employee. To calculate cost per hire, divide the total of all external costs by the total of all internal costs, then multiply by 100.

$$\text{Cost per Hire (\$)} = \frac{\text{Sum Total of All External Costs}}{\text{Sum Total of All Internal Costs}} \times 100$$

PRO TIP

Find out which metrics are more appealing to your stakeholders, such as cost of hiring, time to productivity, time to hire, or results of exit interviews. Stakeholders will be more receptive to metrics that track costs and productivity.

Check-Ins and Interviews

Managers should check in with new and new-to-role employees periodically to make sure their needs are being met and to gather feedback about the onboarding process. In addition, exit and stay interviews also give you valuable information for your onboarding program's evaluation.

TOOL

The "Manager's Check-In Meeting Guides," located at the end of this chapter, provide questions for managers to use after the employee's first 30, 60, and 90 days, to identify additional employee needs and gather feedback about the onboarding process.

Exit Interviews

Conduct exit interviews when employees are leaving the company to learn about their employment experience. Look for trends in the data and track them over time to see how they change. HR usually handles exit interviews using different methods, which have their own advantages and disadvantages (Table 5-4); ask them for the data if you are from another business function. You can use this information to prospectively target issues related to recruitment, selection, and onboarding.

Table 5-4. Advantages and Disadvantages of Exit Interview Methods

Method	Advantage	Disadvantage
In Person by HR	• Get more information • Give a personal touch	• Employee concerns about confidentiality • May be too time consuming • Easy to lose information if not documented
Telephone Exit Interviews by HR or External Consultants	• Probe for information in each question • Enter data in the HR system as it is collected • Easier to schedule	• Time consuming • Expensive if conducted by outside consultants • Employee may resist sharing negative information
Paper and Pencil Surveys	• Takes less time to complete than interviews • Employees may share more information than in interviews	• Time consuming to collect and tabulate data • Individual handwriting may be difficult to read and interpret
Online Exit Interview Management Systems	• Easy to administer • Information is automatically tracked and compiled • Reports are easily available • Higher participation rates than interviews	• Employees may find it impersonal • Participants may use the system to vent • Level of skills in using system may influence level of detail in responses

TOOL

Use the "Guide for Exit Interviews," located at the end of this chapter, to pick and choose questions to use.

Stay Interviews

Conduct stay interviews or surveys to find out why employees stay with the company. Ask how your company's onboarding contributed to their decision to stay. These are questions that managers ask, so provide a tool that is structured and easy to use in a conversational manner. By doing so, you will increase the likelihood that they meet with their employees to discuss these issues and get the information you need to make more informed decisions about what to continue doing in your company's onboarding program and what you should stop doing.

With all the data that you have already collected and converted into meaningful information, you are ready for the next step: communicating the results to inform future actions about your company's onboarding program.

TOOL

Use the "Guide for Stay Interviews," located at the end of this chapter, to gather valuable information about why employees want to stay in the company and its relationship with onboarding.

Communicating Evaluation Results

Communicating results is key to the sustainability of the program because when management and other stakeholders understand the value of onboarding, they become committed to the program. Some benefits of communicating evaluation results include credibility for the program, the opportunity to make program improvements or changes, and the ability to share the program's successes with others, which will include how onboarding affects business outcomes.

Before selecting which metrics you will communicate, identify how you will get the information (refer back to Tables 5-1, 5-2, and 5-3). Then, decide who will receive the results (for example, the company's top management, the board of directors, or the business owners).

You need to determine the best spokesperson for the communications—you need someone who can influence others about the value of metrics and evaluation and turn them into onboarding champions. You also need to find out who won't support the measurement and evaluation process so you can anticipate their needs as you guide them to becoming program advocates. As always, speak the

TOOL

The "Structure for Evaluation Report and Presentation," located at the end of this chapter, provides a starting point for your communication.

language of your audience and the business while establishing connections between those metrics and the business objectives and strategy.

PRO TIP

When you organize your findings for your audience, connect your data to monetary data. Consider what's most relevant for the audience regardless of whether it is positive (for example, increases in revenue) or negative (for example, decrease in customer service satisfaction indices). Introducing department business results before and after the onboarding program will get the attention of senior managers.

As you plan how to communicate results, ask yourself the following questions:

- **What will you communicate?** This question defines the content of the communications and should be answered with a specific timeframe in mind. For instance, will you report orientation evaluation results or stay interview results? Will you discuss increases in cost per hire or changes in turnover?

- **How will the information be communicated?** This question refers to the format that you use to convey the information. For instance, orientation evaluation results are best suited for tables or graphs, while stay interview results are usually summarized using a bulleted list organized by topics. Increases in cost per hire or changes in turnover can be presented using tables or graphs, depending on audience preferences.

- **What are they expecting?** This question requires some homework to align what the audience expects with what you can provide. For instance, are they expecting a presentation or a group discussion? Are they expecting to receive the information before the meeting so that they can ask questions? How much time will they have and what is their average attention span? Do they understand the scope of your evaluation? Are they expecting an analysis of trends and recommendations? Always anticipate their needs as much as you can to sustain the buy-in you obtained with your business case.

- **Who will communicate the information?** This question targets the best person to convey the message to your target audience to get the desired effect. In general, employees prefer to receive information that affects them directly from their immediate supervisors and managers; however, they prefer to receive general information about the business from top management. Executives and boards of directors prefer to hear presentations from a senior professional or leader for decision making.

- **Who is your target audience?** You will focus your entire communication plan based on your audience. Even though the general message may be the same, the level of detail you present and the complexity you include will depend significantly on the audience. For instance, senior management and boards of directors will be more interested in financials, while managers and supervisors will be more interested in examples and quotes from surveys and interviews. More general employee audiences will want to see how they are contributing to the success of the program in specific terms.

PRO TIP

Align the tactics you use to communicate with your company's culture. Use quantitative methods and qualitative methods. Be formal or informal depending on your company's way of doing business.

Make Measuring a Practice

Measurement and evaluation of onboarding programs must become a common business practice. Companies need to be consistent in what and how they measure the year-over-year impact of the changes on methods, processes, revenue, and other business outcomes from onboarding programs. Measure the right things to keep programs fresh and employees engaged.

In the next chapter, we discuss what you need to consider to ensure the sustainability of your program.

Questions to Explore

- What evaluation methods are you most comfortable using?
- Why should your company evaluate its onboarding program?
- What would you measure and evaluate in your company's onboarding program?

- How will your company connect the results of its onboarding program to its business results?
- How do you identify what you need to measure in your onboarding program?
- Do your company's stakeholders differentiate between metrics, measurement, and evaluation?
- What benefits do you see in evaluating your onboarding program?
- Which measures or indicators will you use to evaluate the pre-onboarding? General onboarding? Role-specific onboarding?
- Does your company check in on the progress of onboarded employees before the end of their first year? If yes, how? What can you do differently?
- How do you monitor the support that the buddy/mentor/coach gives the onboarded employee?
- How will you communicate the results of your onboarding program's evaluation?

Tools for Support

Evaluation Forms

Adapt these evaluation forms to help evaluate different stages of the onboarding program. Here you'll find an orientation evaluation form for employees to fill out, as well as 30 and 90 day feedback forms for employees to complete.

Orientation Feedback Form

Name: _____ Date:_____

Department:_____

Manager: _____ Start Date: _____

Rate each statement on a scale of 1 through 5 (1 = strongly disagree and 5 = strongly agree)	
Statement	**Rating**
I am satisfied with the orientation process.	
The amount of time was adequate for the information received.	
As a result of the orientation, I have a better understanding of the:	
• company culture	
• products	
• services	
The information received was _____ at this stage of the onboarding process.	
• relevant	
• beneficial	
• useful	
Other Questions	
What was the best part of the employee orientation?	
What part of the orientation process didn't you like?	

What aspects of the orientation exceeded your expectations?

What part of the employee orientation did you like the most?
- online
  » why?
- face-to-face session
  » why?

Additional Comments:

30-Day Onboarding Feedback

Name: _____	Date:_____

Department:_____

Manager: _____	Start Date: _____

Rate each statement on a scale of 1 through 5
(1 = strongly disagree and 5 = strongly agree)

Statement	Rating
I am satisfied with the past 30-day onboarding process.	
The amount of information received was effective.	
As a result of the 30-day onboarding, I have a better understanding of:	
• my role	
• my department	
• what is expected of me	

Other Questions

What was the best part of the 30-day onboarding process?

What part of the onboarding process didn't you like?

What aspects of the onboarding exceeded your expectations?

What part of the onboarding did you like the most?
• online
  » why?
• face-to-face session
  » why?

Additional Comments:

90-Day Onboarding Feedback

Name: _____ Date:_____

Department:_____

Manager: _____ Start Date: _____

Rate each statement on a scale of 1 through 5 *(1 = strongly disagree and 5 = strongly agree)*	
Statement	**Rating**
I am satisfied with the past 90-day onboarding process.	
I understand my job duties and responsibilities.	
My job matched the job description.	
I feel comfortable talking with my peers.	
The information received was useful.	
Other Questions	
What was the best part of the last 90 days?	
What part of the last 90 days didn't you like?	
What aspects of the past 90 days exceeded your expectations?	
Additional Comments:	

Sample Onboarding Survey

Use an onboarding survey to gain useful information without overburdening participants. Adapt the sample to work for your program.

To help us improve our onboarding program, please answer the following questions.

Questions	Feedback
After the onboarding program, do you have the tools and resources to do your job?	
Do you feel welcomed? Explain.	
As a result of the onboarding program, do you connect with the company? How?	
Which training session engaged you more? Explain.	
Is our training interesting? Interactive?	
What part of the onboarding program has been the most beneficial? Why?	
Do we make it easy to get information?	
What do we need to remove from the onboarding program?	
What do we need to include in the onboarding program?	
Which areas do we need to improve? Explain.	
Which session was more engaging: face-to-face or online?	
Do we have an effective onboarding program? Explain.	

Additional Comments:

Name (optional): _____

Department: _____

Date: _____

Thanks for sharing your feedback!

Sample Email to Accompany the Onboarding Survey

Adapt this sample email to send with your survey request.

To: New Employee
Cc:
Bcc:
Subject: Onboarding Survey

Dear **[Employee Name]**,

We hope that your first 30 days of employment have been a positive and rewarding experience.

To help us ensure a successful onboarding experience, please complete a quick online survey. The survey will take less than 10 minutes to complete and the information will be used to improve our program.

Open the following link: www.OnboardingSurvey.com.

We look forward to your comments. Thank you for your feedback.

Manager's Check-In Meeting Guides

The following are sample questions managers can use to guide 30-, 60-, and 90-day check-in meetings with their onboarded employees.

30 Days

- So far, is the job what you expected it to be? How challenged are you feeling?
- Do you have a good understanding of your role? Why or why not?
- Do you have the information, tools, and resources for success?
- How comfortable are you with the company in general? What about with your department?
- What challenges are you expecting in your job? How do you envision me assisting you with them?
- Do you already feel productive and effective in your role? Why or why not?
- Can you give me examples of learning experiences that would contribute to your success?
- How are things going with your buddy or mentor?
- Are you receiving the feedback and support you need from me?
- How has the onboarding program helped you reach your milestones?

60 and 90 Days

- What areas, tasks, or projects are you enjoying the most within your position?
- What competencies and skills have you acquired or strengthened since you started in your position? Which would you like to develop or strengthen?
- What are you not enjoying as much about your job? Can you share why? What barriers are you encountering?
- How is your onboarding going? What have been the most and least beneficial components?

Guide for Exit Interviews

Use the following questions to gather valuable information about the employee's experience. The questions are grouped into two categories: those for employees who've been with the company for less than a year and those for employees who stayed for longer than a year.

If the employee leaves before the first year of employment, ask:

- Were the duties and demands of your job described accurately during the interview or onboarding processes?
- Did you participate in role-specific onboarding for your function?
- How would you assess the quality of your general onboarding? How about your role-specific onboarding?
- Were your expectations about your job met? If yes, how? If no, why?
- What improvements can you suggest to the organization in terms of recruitment, selection, onboarding, your division, your department, and your job?

If the employee leaves after the first year of employment, ask:

- What was the biggest factor that led you to accept the new job or position?
- What did you like most and least about your job?
- How would you describe the culture of our company?
- If you could change anything about your job or the company, what would it be?
- Management is often a key factor in an employee's decision to leave a company. Were you satisfied with the way you were managed?
- How can our company improve its training and development program?
- What skills and qualifications do you think we need to look for in your replacement?
- Would you consider returning to work here in the future? In what area or function would you consider working?
- What could we do to improve?
- Are there any other issues that you would like us to address?
- What other comments can you share?

Guide for Stay Interviews

Use these questions during stay interviews to learn why employees want to stay in the company and if that was influenced by their onboarding experience.

- What do you look forward to when you come to work?
- What do you like most or least about working here?
- What keeps you working here?
- If you could change something about your job, what would that be?
- What would make your job more satisfying?
- Can you mention the most challenging aspects of your current job situation?
- Do you feel fully utilized in your current role? What talents are you not using?
- What would you like to learn here?
- What motivates (or demotivates) you?
- What can we do to support you?
- What can I do more of or less of as your manager?
- Have you ever thought about leaving the company? If so, why? Why did you decide to stay?

Structure for Evaluation Report and Presentation

Use this list as a starting point to collect and organize information for your evaluation report.

- **Program description:** brief overview of the onboarding program
- **What you did:** the activities that you completed (such as interviews, surveys, and focus groups)
- **Who participated:** how many and from which groups, but don't identify specific individuals
- **Questions:** an example of the guiding questions or survey
- **Results:** shown in tabular, graphic, or other appropriate format, based on the data and audience
- **Findings and trends:** analysis of the results and trends if applicable
- **Recommendations and next steps:** what you propose the company should do with this information and your requests for the onboarding program

Additional Resources

Bailey, A. n.d. *The Kirkpatrick/Phillips Model for Evaluating Human Resource Development and Training.* www.buscouncil.ca/busgurus/media/pdf/the-kirkpatrick-phillips -evaluation-model-en.pdf.

Bauer, T.N. 2010. *Onboarding New Employees: Maximizing Success.* Alexandria, VA: Society for Human Resource Management Foundation.

Bradt, G.B., J.A. Check, and J.A. Lawler. 2016. *The New Leader's 100-Day Action Plan: How to Take Charge, Build or Merge Your Team, and Get Immediate Results,* 4th ed. Hoboken, NJ: John Wiley & Sons.

Bradt, G.B., J.A. Check, and J.E. Pedraza. 2009. *The New Leader's 100-Day Action Plan: An Onboarding Process for Leaders at Every Level,* 2nd ed. Hoboken, NJ: John Wiley & Sons.

Dávila, N., and W. Piña-Ramírez. 2013. *Cutting Through the Noise: The Right Employee Engagement Strategies for You.* Alexandria, VA: ASTD Press.

Eckerson, W.W. 2009. "Performance Management Strategies: Understanding KPIs." KPI Components, August 1. https://tdwi.org/articles/2009/08/01/performance -management-strategies-understanding-kpis.aspx.

Filipkowski, J., M.F. Heinsch, and A. Wiete. 2017. *New Hire Momentum: Driving the Onboarding Experience.* Signature Series: An HCI Insight Partnership. www.hci.org /files/field_content_file/2017%20Kronos_0.pdf.

Fitz-enz, J., and B. Edison. 2002. *How to Measure Human Resource Management,* 3rd ed. New York: McGraw-Hill Education.

HR Daily Advisor. 2017. *2017 Strategic Onboarding Survey Report.* Silkroad. http://hr1 .silkroad.com/strategic-onboarding-survey.

Korn Ferry. 2017. "Korn Ferry Futurestep Survey: 90 Percent of Executives Say New Hire Retention an Issue." Korn Ferry press release, March 21. www.kornferry.com /press/korn-ferry-futurestep-survey-90-percent-of-executives-say-new-hire-retention -an-issue.

Lauby, S. 2017. "Interview: Dr. Jac Fitz-enz on Human Capital Metrics." HR Bartender, September 10. www.hrbartender.com/2017/strategy-planning/jac-fitz-enz-human -capital-metrics.

Maurer, R. 2015. "Onboarding Key to Retaining, Engaging Talent." Society for Human Resource Management, April 16. www.shrm.org/resourcesandtools/hr-topics/talent-acquisition/pages/onboarding-key-retaining-engaging-talent.aspx.

———. 2018. "Employers Risk Driving New Hires Away With Poor Onboarding." Society for Human Resource Management, February 23. www.shrm.org/resourcesandtools/hr-topics/talent-acquisition/pages/employers-new-hires-poor-onboarding.aspx.

Meister, J.C., and K. Willyerd. 2010. *The 2020 Workplace: How Innovative Companies Attract, Develop, and Keep Tomorrow's Employees Today.* New York: Harper Business.

Murphy, M. 2012. *Hiring for Attitude: A Revolutionary Approach to Recruiting Star Performers With Both Tremendous Skills and Superb Attitude.* New York: McGraw-Hill.

Peterson, A. 2016. "The Hidden Costs of Onboarding a New Employee." Glassdoor, September 7. https://glassdoor.com/employers/blog/hidden-costs-employee-onboarding-reduce.

Phillips, J.J., and P.P. Phillips. 2002. "How to Measure the Return on Your HR Investment: Using ROI to Demonstrate Business Impact." *Strategic HR Review* 1(4).

Phillips, J.J., P.P. Phillips, and K. Smith. 2016. *Accountability in Human Resources Management: Connecting to Business Results,* 2nd ed. New York: Routledge.

Sheridan, K. 2012. *Building a Magnetic Culture: How to Attract and Retain Top Talent to Create an Engaged, Productive Workforce.* New York: McGraw-Hill.

SHRM (Society for Human Resource Management). 2016. "Average Cost per Hire for Companies Is $4,129, SHRM Survey Finds." SHRM press release, August 3. www.shrm.org/about-shrm/press-room/press-releases/pages/human-capital-benchmarking-report.aspx.

Sullivan, J. 2002. *HR Metrics the World Class Way.* Peterborough, NH: Kennedy Information.

6

Planning Next Steps:
Where Do You Go From Here?

In This Chapter

- Achieving program sustainability
- Looking out for program roadblocks and barriers
- Exploring options for ongoing learning
- Understanding online onboarding

Program Sustainability

The previous five chapters have taken you through what you need to do to have a successful employee onboarding program. After such an investment of time and resources, you want to ensure the long-term sustainability of the program to benefit the business. Employee onboarding has to become part of the company culture through consistency in delivery and communications for sustainability.

Chapter 5 introduced one of the most critical issues for the program's long-term sustainability: measurement and evaluation of results. Your company can only make informed decisions about the future of the program based on compelling data presented in meaningful ways.

Onboarding program accountability is important because nothing happens in organizations if no one assumes ownership. Powerful positive onboarding results will promote the involvement of key stakeholders in the process and foster the participation of other employees as onboarding becomes integrated into the company's culture.

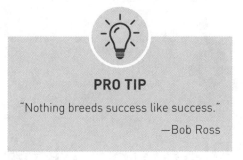

PRO TIP

"Nothing breeds success like success."

—Bob Ross

Assuming program ownership also means anticipating and mitigating roadblocks.

Onboarding Sustainability Roadblocks

It's important to watch out for roadblocks and barriers as you move forward with your program into the future. Let's look at a few you may run into.

Change and Uncertainty

Organizational changes and uncertainty become a barrier for program sustainability because they can cause the company infrastructure on which you based your program to disappear. Any time changes occur, the content of your onboarding program has to reflect them, which leads to rework.

Other possibilities include program stakeholders and participants who supported the program assuming new roles or leaving the organization on short notice. To combat these changes, it's important to constantly emphasize the program's value so you maintain top management's buy-in. Expanding your cadre of resources who deliver the program by selecting and preparing additional facilitators will help if some of your facilitators leave the company.

It's important to keep all resources and stakeholders up-to-date on the latest onboarding program revisions so that they convey the correct message to program attendees. Take additional steps to be prepared for last-minute changes that affect the program; even though they are beyond your control, these changes could cause a negative impression on new or new-to-role employees.

Lack of Long-Term Support

If onboarded employees aren't supported in their role long term, it can result in employee disappointment, which can lead to disengagement and decisions to leave the organization. Onboarding programs have to go beyond the formal group sessions, individual meetings, and training sessions. When companies don't set up an infrastructure to support onboarded employees in the long run, they are more likely to feel isolated and abandoned. Your organization can support employees without incurring extraordinary expenses by maximizing the resources that they already have and increasing managers' awareness of the importance of enabling employee success. Monitor progress consistently.

First Impressions

Underestimating the power of a new employee's first impression can make companies come across as if they disregard their brand. Sometimes companies wrongly assume they can erase the consequences of errors or oversights during onboarding. However, employees are very vulnerable during their first days at work because they are undergoing a major transition. Thus, they are more likely to misinterpret cues and make assumptions based on the limited information they are receiving because they lack points of reference and comparison to reach their own conclusions. Give special attention to every detail to ensure that it reinforces the brand to achieve the desired effect.

Providing an Incomplete Company Picture

Limiting the scope of involvement and participation in the onboarding program to one or two company functions, rather than the organization as a whole, gives new employees an incomplete picture of the company and what it values. When onboarding programs, especially general onboarding, present a limited view of an organization's departments and functions, employees aren't able to appreciate the full scale of the operation they joined. This restricts and delays potential contributions beyond their units until they can obtain the information on their own. Individual differences in employee competencies and aptitudes may mitigate or exacerbate the negative effects of this shortsightedness. Make onboarding inclusive across the organization. Remember the "WOW!" effect.

Ignoring the Learning Curve

Underestimating the importance of the employee's learning curve to meet performance standards places the employee at a disadvantage. Onboarding allows companies to establish a level playing field for employees to meet performance standards. Even though onboarding, especially at the role-specific level, typically shortens the time that employees need to achieve performance standards, it is not a quick fix that will accelerate productivity. Account for the learning curve of each position for every employee to reach the desired performance level.

Lack of Support From Managers' Direct Reports

A manager's direct reports will influence their success or failure in delivering results because managers work through others. In general, it is in the direct reports' best interest to have a successful manager. Therefore, they will likely be aligned with the manager's vision for the future and facilitate cultural assimilation by providing useful insights and feedback.

However, if some of a new manager's direct reports have a longer tenure with the company, whether they are new to the company or to the role, any informal alliances they have forged over the years will influence the level of support from others in the team positively or negatively. Those who were interested in the position, but were passed over, may resent the new manager. Former peers who are now direct reports may not understand the need to shift behaviors or may insist on maintaining a relationship that can't exist anymore. HR and L&D need to support the new manager in handling these issues promptly to reduce the likelihood of long-term repercussions. The manager's career and the business depend on their swift action.

A New Manager's Peers

The influence of a new manager's peers will pave the way for their smooth assimilation into the role. While most learning and acculturation will come from experience, the new manager will need a reference group to adopt behaviors and points of view consistent with the company culture and with the manager subculture. This reference group can become a source of support and information about the business, its history, and its future. They know and have gone through what it takes to perform the role. HR and L&D have to be ready to address any potential conflicts that may arise. Internal politics always need to intervene in these interactions, particularly if some of the new manager's peers perceive any career threats from the new manager.

Issues With Other Employees

Other employees within the department can become the company's cultural ambassadors, but they need preparation to understand the role. These employees can either become a source of support for onboarded employees or a major barrier for their success because they interact with individual contributors whether they work at the same location or remotely. In those daily interactions, these employees transmit many of the unwritten rules of behavior of the department and company. They can also point the onboarded employee in the right direction to find solutions and provide introductions to start building important relationships within and outside the department. Managers and HR have to anticipate and address any misalignments and political issues with these employees before their actions become a major challenge for the onboarded employee, the department, and the company.

TOOL

Use the "Onboarding Program Roadblocks Checklist," located at the end of this chapter, to identify potential challenges that could derail your company's general onboarding or role-specific onboarding program.

Ongoing Learning

Onboarding is the beginning of the employee's learning and development process in the company. Sustaining onboarding implies sustaining employee learning through a carefully orchestrated combination of informal and formal learning experiences that continue after the onboarding program ends.

By continuing the learning experience, you show onboarded employees that the company values them and wants them to have the best learning experience in the organization. It also helps to encourage employees to learn new skills, especially ones that are needed long term within the organization. An employee becomes more engaged when they believe the company values their learning goals.

Table 6-1 lists some suggestions for development activities that employees can do to continue strengthening their skills. They are organized by the groups of employees who would benefit the most from them.

Table 6-1. Suggested Ongoing Development Activities by Group of Employees

Development Activity	Group of Employees			
	Hourly Employees	Individual Contributors	Managers	Executives, Directors, VPs
E-learning programs	X	X		
On-the-job training	X	X		
Information on company website or intranet	X	X	X	
Involvement in professional groups and associations	X	X	X	X
Leadership roles in professional groups and associations			X	X
Informal company social activities	X	X	X	
Formal training programs and workshops (on-site and off-site)		X	X	
Visits to other departments or company locations		X	X	
Virtual communities and support groups		X	X	
Participation in company activities	X	X	X	X
External coaches		X	X	X
Skip-level meetings with key individuals		X	X	X
Formal external training programs focused on legal and financial topics		X	X	X
Leadership tools (e.g., 360-degree assessments)				X
Industry exposure				X
Involvement with boards of directors				X

Online Onboarding

Face-to-face contact in onboarding is irreplaceable. However, we understand that online onboarding is the only option for some companies, especially for general orientation. If companies decide to put their onboarding programs online, we have several recommendations. Companies with online onboarding programs need to:

- Address new employees' learning preferences.
- Include images, pictures, sound effects, and simulations.
- Maintain data and keep information up-to-date.
- Assign an owner to the process.
- Make content and delivery visually appealing.
- Ensure that the programs are truly representative of the organization.

Online onboarding does have some benefits: Companies that automate their onboarding gradually diminish their dependence on printed documents, thus reducing costs. It's also a way to ensure a timely and steady delivery of information when employees need it, which means they are more likely to retain the information.

In online onboarding, everything is presented in more detail because the information is self-explanatory—so adjust the content to the media that you will use. More information is better than less information; however, the key to avoiding overload lies in structuring the delivery of that information in manageable chunks. Before you can create a successful online program, you'll need to thoroughly document everything you plan to include and create scripts—leave nothing to chance. In your scripts, speak to all the typical concerns of new hires upon joining an organization. Repeat and reinforce key messages through different means to make sure that they are understood. Have a plan B so that the program can continue if you encounter any technical problems.

Avoid having to handle the following situation.

Gregory's Story

Gregory is in charge of the company's online onboarding program. Even though the program was initially successful, the situation changed when the company restructured and the program's content was not updated.

Managers and supervisors are saying that the onboarding program is useless because the information is out of date. Gregory has been requesting the information he needs to update the program, but he has not received any responses.

The company's online onboarding program has lost its initial effectiveness. Having support from all stakeholders is key for the program's success. Gregory needs to garner support from key stakeholders whose commitment to the program will ensure that he receives the necessary information to update the material. Keeping stakeholders informed of the program's progress and its impact on business results will sustain the program's positioning as a worthy investment.

Your company may choose to leverage its available technological resources for role-specific onboarding, such as addressing technical and regulatory content; nonetheless, managers still need to be directly involved with their employees.

PRO TIP

If onboarding takes place online, be sure to include the program's essential elements and make it interactive with questions, quizzes, games, and exercises.

Next Steps, Building Relationships

To keep the program alive and strong, the key is consistency. Now you have a road map to follow to revisit that organizational snapshot, create a compelling business case, and justify the company's investment in the program. You will not be starting at square one.

The lessons you learned along the way will be the most useful resources to prepare and launch the next iteration of the program. You know what worked and what did not work to make onboarding successful. You understand what you need to do to get management and other stakeholders involved in general and role-specific onboarding. You have built relationships that will contribute to the success of the program and, most important, to the success of those employees who join the company and believe in what it stands for. You appreciate the value of measuring and evaluating. Onboarding is ongoing.

Questions to Explore

- How do you plan to use what you learned from your program's evaluation to sustain the program?
- How will you handle any organizational changes that may have an impact on the onboarding program?
- Do you have a pool of potential facilitators ready if any current facilitators go elsewhere?
- What is the biggest enabler to onboarding in your company? How will you leverage company resources to optimize them?

- What are the biggest barriers to onboarding in your company? How do you plan to overcome them?
- What elements of online onboarding would be useful to your company? Where would you start?
- What can you do to make a case for the potential benefits of automating some components of your onboarding program?
- Are you ready for the challenge of sustaining the program?

Tools for Support

Onboarding Program Roadblocks Checklist

Use this checklist for the general onboarding program and role-specific onboarding programs by department.

Completed by:			Date:
Potential Roadblocks	Yes	No	Comments
Organizational Changes and Uncertainty			
Lack of Long-Term Support			
Underestimating the Power of First Impressions			
Limiting the Scope of Involvement and Participation in the Program			
Underestimating the Importance of the Employee Learning Curve			
Influence of New Manager's Direct Reports			
Influence of New Manager's Peers			
Influence of Other Employees			

Additional Resources

Ellis, R. 2016. "How to Craft Onboarding That Has Staying Power." ATD Insights, March 7. www.td.org/insights/how-to-craft-onboarding-that-has-staying-power.

Ferrazzi, K. 2015. "Technology Can Save Onboarding From Itself." *Harvard Business Review,* March 25. https://hbr.org/2015/03/technology-can-save-onboarding -from-itself.

Hirsch, A.S. 2017. "Don't Underestimate the Importance of Good Onboarding." Society for Human Resources Management, August 10. www.shrm.org /resourcesandtools/hr-topics/talent-acquisition/pages/dont-underestimate -the-importance-of-effective-onboarding.aspx.

PwC. 2016. *The Future of Onboarding.* PWC Financial Services, December. www.pwc.com /il/he/bankim/assets/pwc-the-future-of-onboarding.pdf.

Acknowledgments

Our books are team efforts. They come to fruition as a result of the contributions and support of many individuals who arrive at the right time.

We would like to thank:

- Ryan Changcoco and Ann Parker for the opportunity to create with you again.
- Kathryn Stafford and Melissa Jones for challenging our thinking.
- L&D and HR professionals for sharing your wisdom for the past year to make this book happen.

Our families, for your unconditional support and endless encouragement:

- Norma: Manuel, Mamma, the Trees and the Support Group at Laderas.
- Wanda: Frank, Nelsi, Iván, Tere, Pedri, Mami (with your new light) and the Support Team at Lelo's.

Our friends, especially:

- Us:
  » The AON Team: Manuel, Eva, and Ivelisse . . .your engagement is priceless.
  » Luis S… you deserve another star.
  » Elaine Biech for believing in us and showing us countless examples of what works.
- Wanda:
  » Magaly . . . it's done
  » Simon . . . friendship matters
  » Ylde . . . NOW it's your turn
  » Alfredo C . . . the writing will continue
- Norma:
  » Patricia … distance does not matter
  » María … caring about what matters
  » Alfredo H … time flies
  » Oscar … doing nothing is doing a whole lot

About the Authors

Norma Dávila is a certified career development strategist who guides clients through targeted introspection and self-assessments to identify strengths and interests before embarking on career changes. Her approach to career coaching positions her clients to gain the self-confidence to present themselves as the best candidate during job interviews. Norma, a certified resume writer by PARW/CC, adapts her advice to best suit client professional experience and aspirations. A firm believer in the value of networks, she steers them to optimize every personal or virtual opportunity to connect with others. A natural talent developer, Norma focuses her practice on entry-level and midcareer professionals across the entire employee life cycle, and has supported employees from industries including banking, technology, telecommunications, pharmaceutical, medical devices, dairy products, aerospace manufacturing, retail sales, risk management, automotive sales, energy, waste management, and funeral services. She is recognized for communicating complex ideas in easy-to-understand terms to all audiences and introducing concrete examples to which they can relate. Norma specializes in designing and delivering learning experiences that lay the groundwork to acquire and strengthen competencies and skills on topics such as team development, business writing, customer service, performance management, employee communications, and transition management. She is a Society for Human Resource Management Senior Certified Professional, and has a bachelor's degree in psychology from Yale University and master's and doctoral degrees in psychology from the University of Chicago.

Wanda Piña-Ramírez is an action-driven, strategic management and executive consultant with a proven track record of contributing to the bottom line in companies spanning from multinational corporations to small businesses located in Puerto Rico, the continental United States, the Caribbean, and Latin America. Her innovative, energetic, and open-minded consulting style is an asset when dealing with ambiguity and challenging business situations. As the longest-serving member of AON Puerto Rico's Mejores Patronos (Best Employers) Committee, she has firsthand knowledge of industries as diverse as restaurants, insurance, medical laboratories, pharmaceuticals, hospitality, professional associations, hospitals, banking, pharmacy information systems, general information processing, refrigeration, medical devices, and building materials. Wanda is certified as a coach from the University of Puerto Rico at Río Piedras, as a practitioner in neurolinguistic programming and applied kinesiology by the International NLP Trainers Association, as a human resources administrator by the Escuela Avanzada de Administración de Recursos Humanos y Legislación Laboral de Puerto Rico, and as a legal intercessor for cases of domestic violence and aggression in Puerto Rico. She is a frequent guest on radio and television programs, where she brings together the legal and business components of talent development and human resources management, tackling such topics as business metrics, labor law, sexual harassment, and domestic violence. Wanda also contributes her expert opinion on the latest issues affecting today's workforce to news outlets and other forums such as professional associations, business groups, and nonprofit organizations.

Wanda and Norma are business partners in The Human Factor Consulting Group, senior consultants for AON, and subject matter experts, program facilitators, and program translators for SHRM specializing in Latin America. They are both certified DDI facilitators, field editors for ATD Links, and co-authors of *Cutting Through the Noise: The Right Employee Engagement Strategies for You* (ASTD Press, 2013) and *Passing the Torch: A Guide to the Succession Planning Process* (ATD Press, 2015). They've also written articles in *TD, T+D, The Public Manager,* and for multiple blogs, and presented at ATD's annual International Conference & Exposition, SHRM's Talent Management Conference, SHRM's Conference Preview Workshops, ATD's México Summit, and Ellevate.

Index